THAT
FINAL
SUMMER

THAT
FINAL
SUMMER

MARGARET SMITH

CHRISTIAN FOCUS PUBLICATIONS

© 1992 Margaret Smith
ISBN 1 871 676 916

Published by
Christian Focus Publications Ltd
Geanies House, Fearn, Ross-shire,
IV20 1TW, Scotland, Great Britain.

Cover illustration
by
Mike Taylor

Cover design
by
Seoris N. McGillivray.

Printed and bound in Great Britain by
Cox & Wyman Ltd, Reading, Berks

and fly away. What was he thinking? Would he tell her he loved her? Or break her heart all over again?

Tom's eyes lit up, and his mouth curved into a delicious smile that set the butterflies fluttering in her stomach. She still didn't know what he would say as he stepped up to her and reached for her hands, wrapped them in his large, warm ones. 'I love you with all my heart, Fi. There's never been anyone else for me since the day I first set eyes on you in the children's ward at Auckland Hospital.'

Happiness spread through her like a tornado, flinging its warm tendrils down to her toes, out to her fingertips, and easing the weight on her heart. 'Thank goodness,' she breathed quietly, and slipped her arms around his neck. 'What took you so long?'

'Sometimes you still are as impatient as ever.'

'Especially when I'm dealing with a certain stubborn man I know.' She brushed his mouth with hers. Suddenly she felt very impatient. 'Where are we going with this? If I stay in Hanmer Springs I've got ideas about what I'll do with my plastic surgery expertise. Ideas that could help fund the hospital, too.'

'You can do whatever you think is best. I just want you back in my life, Fi. That means in every part of it. The hospital, my cottage…my bed.' He kissed the corner of her mouth. 'I'd like to have a family, Fi. With you.'

Fiona's eyes misted over. 'Are you sure? You haven't been able to spare me five minutes most of the week. That's not the sort of marriage I want.' But they were getting darned close.

'I'm absolutely sure. I'm even thinking about getting a manager to take care of all that paperwork I loathe.'

Suddenly she laughed and squeezed him tight. This felt so right. She'd come home. Home to Tom, the man she loved more than life itself. Then they were kissing. And hugging. And kissing some more.

Then just as suddenly she pulled away, looking into those beautiful eyes. 'Tell me again.'

He hauled her back against him. 'I love you, Fiona Saville. Will you marry me?'

She leaned back in his arms, and those swollen lips curved into a wide, heart-stopping smile. 'Shame on you. I'm a married woman.'

EPILOGUE

Two years and nine months later.

FIONA dashed through the gardens towards the new house tucked in amongst the trees and the flowerbeds that Connor's mother tended regularly. She was late.

But she slowed as she came out into the autumn sun. She missed the heat of summer and grabbed whatever sun she could before winter slammed in and created havoc. Freezing cold, icy havoc, that Tom enjoyed and she tolerated. All part of their busy, rich lives—lives they wouldn't change for anything.

Although there was about to be one small change. One Tom knew nothing about yet.

Giggles burst out across the short distance from home and her steps quickened again.

'Mummy, Mummy, here I am. Daddy's been tickling me.'

Fiona reached down and swung her beautiful two-year-old up into her arms and smothered her with kisses. 'Hello, my birthday girl. Are you ready for your party?'

'No one's here yet. The twins *will* come?' Worry clouded Molly's grey eyes.

'Of course they will.' Maddy and Karla wouldn't miss

the party for anything. They adored Molly, had almost adopted her.

Tom stood on the large veranda that ran the length of their new, larger house. 'Come on, you two, stop gossiping. We've got a party to get organised.'

Fiona rolled her eyes at her husband. 'Just what have you been doing all morning if you haven't got everything ready? While I've been working, I might add.'

He grinned at her. 'You can close the plastic surgery unit any time you like, and become a stay-at-home mum.'

'As if.' He knew she loved her work, and enjoyed the fact that the money she made through plastic surgery went towards helping those families who would otherwise struggle to send their children to Tom's hospital. She'd not forgotten Shaun Elliott's parents and the hardship they'd faced to get their son the help he needed.

'The party's ready to go. The barbecue's warming. Just waiting on Kerry and Craig to arrive.' Tom pulled his women in against his chest for a cuddle. 'Molly and I have been having a bit of clean-out of her room.'

'I'm bigger now. I don't want the plastic ducks or the books with no paper.'

The fabric books that Molly had spent hours trying to read. Fiona's heart squeezed. Her baby was growing up fast.

Tom nudged her. 'Thought we could give a box of toys to the kindergarten fundraising stall.'

'Good idea. They'll be grateful for them.'

'And there's the box of baby monitors. All ten of them. I'm sure we could find a home for *them*.'

When they'd learned Fiona had got pregnant that week she'd come to see Tom, Tom had gone shopping for a monitor to put in the crib, ready for the day Molly was born. In an attempt to lighten their fears he'd bought ten. Thankfully not one of them had ever gone off.

CONTENTS

To
my husband Kenny,
and our daughters
Mairie Christine, Karis Ann and Alexandra.

CHAPTER 1

COLD CONTROL

In that moment, his mother was the child, he the grown-up.

"I won't let him do this to you, Mum. No way! I'm going to see him - tonight."

"No, Graham. You mustn't!" His mother's words came out in a tight, terrible voice. "For my sake, please don't go."

The look on her son's face frightened Mary Maclean. It was as if he didn't know her. As if she were another person. Or perhaps, she thought, perhaps for the first time in his seventeen years, he was seeing her as someone who had to be protected. Someone to do battle for. And, with those storm clouds looming over his face, he did look ready to slay at least one dragon!

"I'm going. I've had enough of that toffee-nosed nurd to last me a lifetime. Give me a re-run of what he said, so that I'll have all my facts right."

Mrs Maclean saw the clenched jaws. And she realized that no matter how much she tried, her mind couldn't plumb the depths of the anger and the powerlessness. Her son's facade of cold control didn't hide his feelings.

"Mr Pugh-Smith," she began, "doesn't really have much to do with us domestic staff. His wife is usually the one who discusses menus and stores with me, plus all the other little details of the catering side. And she's the one who gives me the instructions for looking after the Lodge when the family go back to their London home in October."

"So when the Big Boss himself sent for you..." The second half of Graham's statement remained unspoken.

His mother was silent for a moment and her son looked at the gentle, grave face framed in a cloud of soft, dark-brown hair. A warm presence. A widow. A waste? He pushed aside this almost-irreverent thought and let her continue.

"Well, I suppose I should have known it was something Mrs Pugh-Smith didn't want to handle. Anyway, she was busy organising more redecorating."

Her shoulders sagged suddenly. "Mr Pugh Smith said, 'Sorry about your plans for tomorrow, Mrs Maclean. I know you did tell me in ample time, but a few friends of ours will be arriving on the island by plane tomorrow. And we'll be expecting you to excel yourself with those traditional recipes.' He didn't look me in the eye all the time he was talking to me. Not once. Then he said, 'You are *so* good at those type of things, Mrs Maclean.' "

"I'll give him 'so good' - the upper-class twit!"

Mrs Maclean walked across to the peat-fired stove and gingerly opened the oven. The kitchen filled with the good smell of sugar, sultanas and cinnamon as the fruit loaf began to brown. She closed the door and turned to her son.

"When he said all that, I prayed an instant prayer that I wouldn't show anger. I explained to him that Saturday was the only day we could take our peats home, otherwise we wouldn't get our year's supply of fuel. We were already ages behind everyone else in getting them home. And then, on Monday, the men from the village would be starting on that new road and we wouldn't be able to get to the peat banks till the next year again."

"Did he do a Marie Antoinette?"

His mother looked mystified.

"Marie Antoinette, remember? The French Revolution? People starving, begging for bread, and she said, 'Let them eat cake.' Pugh-Smith's equivalent would be 'Buy coal, Mrs Maclean!' "

"Worse than that, actually." She plunged her rubber-gloved hands into a basin of sudsy water and made a great thing of cleaning the hand whisk and bowl. "He said, 'Why don't you take the peats home on Sunday?' "

"Wow! He sure knows how to hit where it hurts, doesn't he? He must know after all these years of coming up here, that you're a committed Christian and that you try to keep

Sunday as a special day."

His mother raised her eyes from her task and zeroed in on that last statement. "Graham, don't start getting self-righteous on me, will you? You certainly don't show that you care much for the Lord, or his day!"

"At least I've got a bit of heart. You couldn't find Pugh-Smith's heart even if you had to cut him wide open with a knife. And anyway, I thought God favoured us poor, not the stinking rich."

His eyes, grey and clear, fringed with a thatch of dark hair, now challenged hers. He had quietly, surely, shown his mother the small, hidden reason behind the big one - that a million miles lay between them and the Pugh-Smiths, and that the chasm could only be bridged by money. Lots of it.

"It's not just his refusal to let me have tomorrow off that's getting to you, is it?" Mrs Maclean asked.

He looked out of the window avoiding her eyes. Outside, the summer was at its glorious green-and-gold peak. Bees tripped drowsily from flower to flower, languid butterflies floated by, and further away he could see the fields dappled with grazing sheep. A few lambs which still hadn't outgrown their adolescence were playing King of the Castle on a bumpy hill.

"No," he said at last. "It's the rotten unfairness of it all."

The remark simply fell and lay there like a log across their path.

"It's so ... unjust," he continued, desperately trying to pin a label on the thing he felt. "Look at us. Badly needing to have our house renovated. Our upstairs windows are just about falling apart, the front door can hardly close because the wood is so warped, there's a crack in the chimney-breast. And we can't do anything about it because over and above the grant we'd get, we would still have to cough up a few thousand.

"Yet, the Pugh-Smiths of this world come waltzing up from their stately homes in England, buy a summer estate here on the Isle of Morna and rake in oodles of grant money for improving property that is in mint condition - at least, compared to ours.

"And, on top of that ... they act like they're doing the rest of the world a big favour by just living. The locals are supposed to show undying gratitude if they're given one of their measly, low-paid jobs on the Estate."

And the words, aching with a long sense of injustice, kept coming.

"Sheleen Pugh-Smith is my age, right? She's going to University; I'm going to College, if my results are okay. That's fine. All things seem equal there. But they're not. She doesn't need to worry her pretty little head about a mother who's struggling to make ends meet. Year in, year out - the same financial grind. I'll go to College with one gigantic guilt complex, because, for the first time in my life, *I* could be earning something for you."

"Graham, please ... " Mary Maclean knew suddenly that her son had opened a door that had been sealed tight.

"Instead, I'll be struggling on a grant and I know you'll be struggling to help me out." He found himself in an intensity of hot bitterness that, for a moment, choked him and made it impossible to continue.

His mother remained silent. She looked out over the sweet, green fields as if she could see things that had happened long, long ago. Or was it in the distant future? "I wish you didn't feel like that," she said at last.

He became silent, withdrawn, realizing that his sense of powerlessness had overwhelmed him. And now he had hurt his mother. Her pleasure, her pride in his academic future had gone. It was all spoiled.

"James - James Munro - he's behind a lot of what you're saying, isn't he?"

"No! Well, maybe. He does make me ... uh, notice things. But I'd have come round to that way of thinking anyway. I would have seen it for myself."

"So that's what you talk about when you both go fishing down at the river."

"That, and other things."

"James is easily embittered, Graham. He collects injustices in the same way that other people collect postage stamps."

"Top stuff, Mum!" Graham retorted with a wintry smile. "Someone here is witty at least."

Mrs Maclean poured out coffee and the bright afternoon sunshine spilled across the table, flooding the coffee mugs and honey jar with burnished gold. She smiled at him, and a dimple appeared at one corner of her mouth. Suddenly everything seemed a little better than it had been.

They sat at the pine kitchen table in an almost companionable silence. The fire-sounds in the stove were barely audible and the old croft house creaked softly in the stillness.

"Graham," Mrs Maclean eventually said, "do you want to know - would you like me to tell you - how I feel about the Pugh-Smiths?"

"Go on, surprise me."

"I feel sorry for them. No, maybe 'sorry' isn't the right word. I feel a real compassion for them. Maybe in this world's hierarchy they're way up at the top of the ladder, but in God's eyes they're poor, needy people with no real meaning to their lives."

"Wow, that's heavy, Mum. Wish *they* could hear all this!"

There was a great meaning in her voice as she said, "There's a lostness about them. Like there is about you ..."

"Back off, Mum. I didn't inherit your faith, you know. It doesn't come with the genes."

"Well, that's one thing we can agree on, my prodigal son." She smiled and sipped her coffee.

He felt that coldness start again somewhere deep inside him. He wanted to stop her before she said anything else. He knew that it was something he did not want to hear. In some small corner of his mind he recognised that her deep faith was something he could not face. It was easier to cope with Pugh-Smith & Co!

He took a gulp of coffee and said, "I'm going."

"No, Graham ... Please don't."

"A man's gotta do what a man's gotta do." His mouth twisted into what might have been a smile. "This is my final, long, summer holiday at home. You know that. And I don't want to look back and be ashamed of it."

With that, he went outside and strode away, the sunshine streaming over him like a banner.

'Tom.' Fiona lifted her head, met his steady gaze. 'Don't take those monitors anywhere. We're going to need them.'

He stared at her, his beautiful, strong mouth curving up into a big smile, the grey of his eyes brightening into a soft ash colour. 'We are?'

'We are. In November.' She stood up on her tiptoes and kissed that smile.

DR ZINETTI'S SNOWKISSED BRIDE
by Sarah Morgan

Medic Meg thought heartbreaker Dr Dino Zinetti would never look twice at a scruffy tomboy like her—but she's got under Dino's skin! This Christmas he'll teach Meg the meaning of romance! But he doesn't expect to receive his own crash-course in love…

THE CHRISTMAS BABY BUMP
by Lynne Marshall

Dreamy doc Phil Hansen knows how to cure new colleague Stephanie Bennett's heartache—a Christmas fling! Dazzled by Phil's charm and long overdue some happiness, Stephanie can't resist. Until their fling throws them a surprise…

CHRISTMAS IN BLUEBELL COVE
by Abigail Gordon

GP Ethan is filled with hope when Francine unexpectedly returns to Bluebell Cove. It will take a good dose of festive cheer and their very own miracle Christmas baby to mend their marriage—and their hearts!

THE VILLAGE NURSE'S HAPPY-EVER-AFTER
by Abigail Gordon

In Bluebell Cove, nurse Phoebe's finally found a place she and her baby can call home. But gorgeous new boss Harry Balfour is having a disturbing effect on her! When Harry realises that Phoebe is one in a million, he wants to make *all* her dreams come true!

**On sale from 5th November 2010
Don't miss out!**

Available at WHSmith, Tesco, ASDA, Eason and all good bookshops
www.millsandboon.co.uk

THE MOST MAGICAL GIFT OF ALL
by Fiona Lowe

Dr Jack Armitage's trip is delayed when an unexpected gift is left on his doorstep…a little girl! His replacement Dr Sophie Norman didn't expect to be a stand-in mummy—but whilst ensuring this little girl has a magical Christmas to remember they find the most magical gift of all: a family.

CHRISTMAS MIRACLE: A FAMILY
by Dianne Drake

In the village of White Elk, Dr James Galbraith needs help from his ex, Nurse Fallon O'Gara. Fallon is only too happy to give it, but she's hiding a heartbreaking secret. As the snow flutters down Fallon finds safety in James's arms, and is finally ready to become mother and wife.

On sale from 5th November 2010
Don't miss out!

Available at WHSmith, Tesco, ASDA, Eason and all good bookshops
www.millsandboon.co.uk

are proud to present our...

Book of the Month

Proud Rancher, Precious Bundle
by Donna Alward
from Mills & Boon® Cherish™

Wyatt and Elli have already had a run-in. But when a
baby is left on his doorstep, Wyatt needs help.
Will romance between them flare as they
care for baby Darcy?

Mills & Boon® Cherish™
Available 1st October

Something to say about our Book of the Month?
Tell us what you think!

millsandboon.co.uk/community
facebook.com/romancehq
twitter.com/millsandboonuk

CHAPTER 2

THAT MAN!

The Lodge door opened. "Yes? Oh, it's ... I've quite forgotten your name, young man."

"Graham Maclean."

The eyes looking at him were hard and blue and old, the voice measured and precise - Mrs Pugh-Smith, Senior. Wider, grudgingly, the door opened.

"If you're looking for your mother, I believe she is off duty. I'm sure you'll find her at your own home."

Graham hated the twist of the thin lips and the subtle sarcasm of the hard English voice. Inside his head, he called her names and felt stupidly pleased.

"I'm sure I *would* find her at her own home. Very sure. In fact, I've just come from there."

"Oh?"

"Who is it, Elisabeth?" The elderly lady's daughter-in-law, Leanda Pugh-Smith, popped her head round the door. An elegant blonde, she spoke in a lazy, laconic way,

15

with the accent of the upper-classes. The gloss of wealth emanated from her whole figure, from the beautifully arranged hair to the perfect oval of her fingernails, and the small, delicate pieces of gold jewellery she wore.

"Graham! How nice to see you!" she beamed, ignoring her mother-in-law's cold barrier of reproof. "Now, I shouldn't say 'How you've grown!' but ... well ... How you've grown! Dark, handsome - and now tall. You must be six feet, at least."

"Only when I tiptoe," Graham smiled.

"Won't you come in?" she asked, smiling warmly to cover the older woman's silence.

"Thanks, I've come to see your ... um, Mr Pugh-Smith."

"I'll let my son know that you're here," Mrs Pugh-Smith, Senior, said in a voice that was clipped and cool. "Although he does not like being disturbed at this time of day."

Graham flashed a glance at the younger woman and saw, to his amusement, his own scorn at this remark mirrored in her eyes. She chatted pleasantly as she led Graham through the thickly-carpeted hallway into the study.

He noticed the walls of leather-bound books, the antique furniture and the oil paintings in their gold leaf frames. An enormous slab of mirror glass filled one wall and seemed to magnify the huge solidity of the mahogany desk.

"Neat," he said.

"I'm glad you like it, Graham. It's my first attempt at Interior Decorating. We always commission a London firm to do any redecorating for us, but, this time, I wanted to try out my own ideas."

"My mother is pretty good at wallpapering, too," Graham remarked, and then realized that, of course, Mrs Pugh-Smith hadn't personally wallpapered the study. She had merely chosen the paper.

He caught onto Mrs Pugh-Smith's words - " ... and I hope Sheleen will be back before you go."

"Sheleen? She's here?" He felt suddenly weak, as if his knees had lost solidity.

"Yes, she flew up yesterday. Didn't your mother tell you?"

"Uh ... no. I thought - I thought Sheleen was giving this place a miss for once. I thought she was going abroad."

"That was her father's idea, but, " she shook her head in wonderment, "she really loves it up here, you know. And this will be her last, long summer holiday here before University, and then work or whatever comes her way. It'll be the same for you, won't it?"

"Yes. I want to pack a lot into this summer. After that, I'll be spending most of my time on the mainland - Edinburgh, I hope."

"How dreadful for your mother."

"Mmmm. Will Sheleen be long? I mean, just now?"

he forced himself to ask. He didn't want to be there when
she did come.

Mrs Pugh-Smith looked at him with a sharp, alert
expression, but before she could reply her mother-in-law
came in to announce that her son would see Graham
briefly in the lounge. She emphasised the word 'briefly'.

Tall and leonine, Jerram Pugh-Smith was pacing the
high-ceilinged lounge in long, slow strides. He was
listening to someone at the other end of the cordless
telephone, and ignored Graham.

Late afternoon sunshine moved into the room and sat
in a corner like an invited guest. Graham watched how
the air coming through the windows stirred the curtains,
making their rich, deep folds drag a little over the carpet
beneath.

Mr Pugh-Smith eventually put down the phone and
said in a loud voice, "Yes? What can I do for you, er,
David?"

"Graham."

"Ah yes, Graham."

His manner was nauseating, Graham thought. As
though a matter of repeating a name was some giant favour
to be grateful for.

"My mother finds it impossible to cancel our plans and
do the catering for the Lodge tomorrow."

Mr Pugh-Smith looked at him in blank astonishment
at first, then the light of remembering came into his eyes.

"Ah yes. Must we go over this well-worn track again!" He turned to Graham, his eyes steady, but there were small points of anger in their depths. "Did your mother not understand what I said this morning?"

"She understood. You didn't."

"I beg your pardon?"

"My mother didn't want me to come here, okay? But I'm sick of the way you treat her. Like some disposable object. Always there when you need her. Looks after the Lodge for you all the year round. Drops everything and comes running when you bring all your huntin', shootin', fishin' friends to the island, even if they arrive by plane at midnight."

"Now, just a minute -"

"She's grateful for the job. She likes it, and I've never heard her complain. Not once - in what? Seven years? Not even when she has to work on Sunday, and she misses the morning service. She makes *one* request to be off, weeks in advance, only to be turned down at the last minute."

"Look, here -" Mr Pugh-Smith began, grim lines forming around his mouth.

"She has no-one to defend her. You know that my father died when I was eight, so she has no one. Except me. I'm not asking for sympathy, Mr Pugh-Smith, just a bit of understanding."

"Understanding?"

"Yes, surely - "

"*You* have to understand that my employees have to fit in with my lifestyle. Not the other way around."

Graham felt almost defeated by his inability to blow up, to blast away, the fastness of the other man's incomprehension. Not just incomprehension, though. "You just don't care enough to try and understand, do you?"

"That's quite enough, young man!" The hard, confident voice jabbed at Graham's eardrums like a finger poked painfully at an abscess. "I may remind you that every year I'm inundated with letters from women, and men - highly qualified cooks - *begging* me for work. So far I have chosen to keep your mother in our employment, because we're satisfied with her standard of cooking. But, rest assured, she would not be hard to replace."

"So, if she wants to keep her job, be at the Estate kitchen tomorrow - is that it?" Graham's voice came out, soft and bitter, but his heart seemed to pump the blood round his body at an alarming rate, a scarlet waterfall surging inside him.

"That is it." With a dismissive half-smile and a wave of his hand, the interview was terminated.

Graham, turning away, felt something he desperately wanted slipping away from him. He felt powerless to hold onto his ability to change things, to make things a little easier for his mother. And his hatred for *that man* was so painful to him that the inside of his chest hurt.

God favouring the poor - what a joke! No wonder his mother hadn't agreed with him when he had said it.

He made his way down the spacious hallway, his thoughts boiling in his head. As soon as he circled through them once, he found he began again, and then again.

"Graham?" A voice stopped him as he passed the study.

"Graham!"

There she was, silhouetted against the window. The afternoon light surrounded her like an aureole, turning her long chestnut hair into tresses of pure copper.

Sheleen. And even through his anger, the ghosts of last summer rose up in his mind.

CHAPTER 3

MISSION ACCOMPLISHED

He moved hesitantly to the door of the study. The smile on Sheleen's face was wide and white and full of pleasure. To Graham it was like being hit with a double bolt of electricity.

"Graham - great to see you again!"

"Oh ... yes. Hi," he said off-handedly.

It was not the way he meant to greet her. Instantly he wished he could do a re-run of the greeting and charge it with warmth and welcome.

The smile faded uncertainly. "How are you? You don't look ... is there anything wrong?"

He stared at the delicately modelled features and saw that those honest green eyes were wide and happy and bewildered and disappointed all at one time.

"No. Should there be?"

"I don't know. You just look as if your life is going down the plug hole, and nobody cares."

"Spot on, Miss Psycho Analyst!" A gleam of humour flickered and faded in his eyes.

"There *is* something wrong. You used to laugh your way out of everything. That's a thing I like about ... "

"It's your father. Someone should crush that guy. Preferably with a rock."

As soon as he heard the words he wished he could recall them, they sounded so harsh and bitter. He saw her flinch as though he had hit her.

She said, "What did he say that was so bad?"

"Where do you want me to start?"

And then, he was flinging his story at her as if daring her to pity him.

"Oh," she said when he had finished. "It sounds familiar. He has to do everything at such an ice-cold level. I guess compassion isn't his strongest asset, is it?"

"Compassion doesn't figure in your father's vocabulary at all, Sheleen."

She seated herself in one of the deep leather armchairs and leaned back as if she were prepared to do a lot of talking, or a lot of listening. For a while, there was silence.

"I've an idea," she eventually began with cool logic. "If we have a buffet, people can help themselves. Your mother doesn't actually need to be there."

"A buffet still needs some preparation, doesn't it?"

"Mmmm. We've got masses of cold cooked meats and

salad stuff here. There's cold salmon and smoked trout, cold roast beef, strawberries and raspberries. And your mother has frozen enough quiches and pastries to feed an army."

"So it's a case of putting it all out on your mile-long dining table and saying 'Stretch or starve'. "

She laughed and he felt he had won a prize. "Something like that!" she said, "Only your mother will still have to come in late tonight or early tomorrow."

"No problem. Tractor plus driver are on hire from ten o'clock in the morning."

"Right. Do you want me to work on my father just now, before you go?"

He didn't reply, savouring the sensation that the day seemed new and alive once more.

"Okay!" she said. "I take it that means 'Yes'." With a quick "Wish me luck" she was gone.

The tight knot of anger inside him loosened. Sheleen was back, so - to pot with her old man. Perhaps ... perhaps they could pick up where they left off last summer. A friendship, unplanned as the doodles on his school jotters, bordering on something deeper. So, perhaps ...

The soft thud of running feet in the hallway broke into his consciousness. Seven year old Timothy Pugh-Smith came to a sudden halt beside Graham and stood, still panting as if he had come a long way and was on the verge of saying something really important.

"Hi, small guy," Graham tweaked his ear playfully, "How're you doing? Still being fed on rocket fuel, aren't you!"

"I ran all the way when I heard you were here," the little boy panted.

He was blonde like all the Pugh-Smiths, apart from Sheleen; and had his mother's face cast into a boyish mould. A thin child with macaroni stick arms and blue, too-big eyes, that he seemed to have inherited from his paternal grandmother.

"Graham, has Glenn had her babies yet?"

"Yeah, four. They all look like their mum. Black and white coats; friendly, inquisitive brown eyes."

"Please, please, can I have one? I've never had a pup of my own. Please, do say yes!" The little boy gave a squeak of excitement and danced a jig around Graham.

"Well, I don't mind giving you one, small guy. I've only managed to give away two so far. But - what will your father say? I don't think he'll be madly keen on a collie, especially a Heinz 57 Variety like this one."

"Don't care. I don't want those horrid Pointer dogs we've got here. I want Glenn's pup."

"Okay, suits me. Tell you what, there's one that's very special. He's got a clownish white face, and he drools all over you when he licks you. You won't need to wash your face the whole holiday."

The little boy's face lit up, but his requests hadn't dried

up yet. "And will you take me fishing on the river? I've got my own rod this year."

"Sorry, no chance. I go there with James." He almost added, 'and he can't stand rich little English boys.'

Timothy drooped with disappointment. He looked so small and sad that Graham felt instantly guilty. He had a soft spot for this, the youngest Pugh-Smith. Charles, the middle one of the family, had fifty thousand subtle ways of annoying people and Graham was glad that he preferred to stay with his grandparents in the South of England.

"Please, Graham, I just like being with you," Timothy pleaded again.

Who could resist that? Graham was beaten. "Okay, tell you what - we'll start off by going fishing for newts. There's a small pool not too far from here. Don't bother to bring your rod; I'll tell you when we'll go."

Graham felt duty-bound to protect himself from the inevitable jealousy he would feel at seeing the 'small guy's' fishing paraphernalia.

Sheleen appeared in the room, with a broad smile and dancing eyes.

"Mission failed?" Graham teased.

"Thanks for the vote of confidence, sir!" she laughed. "He agreed, if your mum comes in for a little while tonight, and then early tomorrow morning."

"Wow!" He smiled, the expression slowly broadening

over his features till they were transformed into a beaming mask of happiness. And then, "Was it hard in the lions' den?"

"A bit."

"How much a bit?"

"About nine on the Richter scale?" She smiled ruefully and fondly ruffled her little brother's hair. "Now, if it had been you doing the asking, little fellow, there would be no problem."

"How d'you mean? Charles might be spoilt, but not this fellow," Graham said, conveniently forgetting that 'this fellow' had neatly twisted him around his little finger.

"It's just that Granny was there too. And I've never been her Flavour of the Month. Don't know why. Maybe she's one of those women who think that sons - and grandsons - are all that matter. Whatever it is, she's got no time for me."

"Ah-hah, a guy wouldn't need to be Einstein to understand that. She can't cope with your seventeen year-old prettiness!"

"Hey, I've got my self-image to maintain here!" she joked. "What about my almost-Mensa intelligence, my razor wit, my appealing modesty ... ?"

They both laughed, Timothy joining in but not understanding that the goofy laughter was more due to relief of tension than to witty comments.

"Help, is that the time?" Graham said, hearing the

chimes of the wall clock. "By now, my mother will have worn out her knees praying for me!"

"So, was it her prayers or your action that resolved your problem, Graham?" Sheleen challenged him.

"Huh? Oh well, we'd have got exactly nowhere if I hadn't come here. And yet Mum didn't want me to go. So I'll chalk up the score for this one."

"Hang on a minute," Sheleen said in a mock-injured voice. "You're forgetting that it was my intervention that saved the day. Who knows ... perhaps it was your mum's prayers that brought *that* about?"

"As you say, Sheleen, who knows? But all that 'turn the other cheek' stuff is strictly for wimps. That's my opinion."

"That's not fair, Graham. No one in their right mind could call your mother a wimp."

"Suppose not," Graham admitted, remembering the unwimp-like row he had been on the receiving end of that very morning. His mother had spared no verbal expense in describing the insanitary conditions of his bedroom.

"Your mother doesn't need a whole lot of people telling her that she's great, okay, popular, and so on. She's the most self-contained person I know. No, self-contained is the wrong word, because she can reach out to another person in a way nobody else can. But - what I mean is - she doesn't seem to rely on other peoples' opinion of herself. She's sure of what she is, and she's happy with it. That's more than most of us can say!"

"Strange to hear you talk of my mother like that, Sheleen. I never thought of her in that way. Or in any other way. She was always - just my mother. Always there. I never *had* to think about her. At least ... "

Her nod encouraged him to go on.

"At least, not till today. I saw her as a person in her own right. A widow, youngish, and this summer having to sort out her feelings about me. Loving and leaving and letting go ... and all that jazz."

"Must be hard. Has she ever thought of marrying again?"

"Marrying again?" He smiled vacuously as if he were amused. "Help, no. She's far too independent now. Can't imagine her buckling down to a relationship where a husband would tell her not to worry her pretty little head about the electricity bill, or the leaking tap, or the bugs in the cabbage plot. No, she's been the boss for too long now."

"Mmmm."

"Look, I've gotto go. See you - very soon?"

"Sure, very soon! Oh, tell your mother that Samuel Stern is coming tomorrow. He's my father's accountant."

"And he has all my sympathy!" Graham grinned. With that, he left the Lodge and plunged into the sunny and magical afternoon, carrying his gladness with him like a concealed treasure.

CHAPTER 4

CHOREOGRAPHY AND CAPITALISM

For Graham, the up-beat feeling was still there next day as he filled the tractor-loads of peat. Out on the moorland, several miles from his home, the feeling was everywhere. It was in the hot blue day, and in the soft sound of the gossiping river water. It was in the miles of moorland and lochs leading to infinity, and in the clear canopy awning of the sky. After the endless, dark and depression-swept winter, the high summer brought a feeling of exhilaration amongst the island community.

James Munro and Graham watched the tractor-driver manoeuvring with the care and swift skill that seemed inborn in every male islander. They had lived with this ritual a long time and knew how to avoid being bogged down in the more treacherous areas. Men, women and tractor then moved along the peat banks as if it had all been arranged by a master choreographer, the pace steady, the team work co-ordinated.

"Great weather for taking home peats," James commented.

"Not so good for fishing, though," Graham said. "But maybe, tonight. Hey, won't you look at that!"

They watched the spot where the river was flowing bank high, its foaming water peat-stained.

"There, look!" And there it was; a glimmering silver bar of salmon leaped clear of the swirling current, hung etched in all its splendour for a moment and then was gone.

"What a beauty! Great to think that some things in life are still free," James enthused. "Not *all* the rivers in this area belong to the Puke-Smiths."

Graham smiled at this. James, he thought, was original, good-looking, interesting, full of life and colour. After a flunked year at University, his philosophy verged on Marxism. And the nearest capitalist he could vent his anger on was Jerram Pugh-Smith.

They watched the tractor thread its way homeward, its burden heavy. A flight of wild geese passed overhead in a big victory sign. They seemed to fly right into the heart of the afternoon sunshine.

Graham and James sat apart from the others, drinking coke and talking of inconsequential things. Then they mulled over the attitude of Jerram Pugh-Smith towards Mrs Maclean's request.

"Typical!" James snorted, a sudden anger surfacing

quickly. "Still that bland sure assumption that they're much better than everyone else. Tell me, how is your mother supposed to think about herself? Is she, or are you, or me, supposed to think we get inferior treatment because we *are* inferior?

" I never thought of myself as inferior to anyone - till I got that holiday job in the estate stables last year. The cold way Puke-Smith and his ancient prune of a mother spoke to me! As if they were seeing past me all the time. They never saw me as a person in my own right. Not as an individual. Just as the machine to muck out the stables."

"I know what you mean. You're treated as an inferior. And then you begin to think, well, maybe I am ... "

James pulled deeply on his cigarette, exhaling a sigh with the smoke. "They don't know anything, do they? And they don't know that they don't know anything. They think that we're not aware of the injustice of it all - the top 10% of this country owning 80% of the wealth. Do you think that's fair? Do you?"

"Uh ... no, I suppose not," Graham said.

"A chip on the shoulder can get to be a heavy load, boys," his mother broke in gently. They had been unaware of her approaching presence.

"Very funny, Mum. This is serious," Graham said. Yet, he felt a vague sense of shame for forgetting that Sheleen was, after all, part of the system he so bitterly resented.

"Heard about the way you were treated yesterday,

32

Mrs Maclean." James fiercely ground the half-smoked cigarette under his heel. "Someone should give Puke-Smith a bit of grievous bodily harm. If I were you, I would do as little as possible for him from now on."

"I don't think you and I see things in quite the same way, James," Mrs Maclean answered. The smile that quietly touched her lips was almost a gesture of gratitude. "You see, I don't see myself as only working for an employer. I try to do everything - for the Lord."

"Aha! Religion is the opiate of the people," James quoted. "Keeps the working class submissive."

"Don't tell me those antiquated ideas are still doing the rounds!" A teasing note floated into her voice.

Graham looked at his mother in surprise. He asked, "What do you mean?"

"They've tossed that philosophy out in Eastern Europe now, haven't they? And remember, Christianity grew in leaps and bounds under Communist regimes of organised godlessness. You see, people - everywhere - have a God-shaped vacuum in their lives. Only God can fill that vacuum. That's not an original thought, by the way. But it's true."

"What about the injustices?" James was stung to protest. "There are things we can change, now."

"Now. I remember, when I was your age, James, wanting things 'now'. Teenagers, and perhaps more than teenagers, set goals for themselves - "

"Heavy stuff, Mum," Graham said. "And I thought these books from the library were just for pressing flowers!"

She went on as if he hadn't spoken. "People want problems resolved *now*, don't they? They want seven-minute chips, one-hour photo developing, instant solutions. Instant happiness."

"So what's wrong with that, Mrs Maclean?" James asked.

"Nothing, in itself. But not when they believe that a pain-free, fun-filled life equals happiness. It doesn't. I should know. 'I have learnt, in whatsoever state I am in, to be content.' "

"Stop trotting out texts, Mum. I've decided I'm an agnostic, remember?" Graham said, his voice sharpening.

"Graham, statements like 'I'm an agnostic', or 'I'm an atheist' - they're nothing more than negative responses to what every person, deep inside, knows to be true. Just like I said before, God is, and we are made for him."

"My mother is trying to indoctrinate me with all this heavy stuff before I go to College," Graham explained to James, in an attempt to cover up his own embarrassment.

His mother looked reflectively across the moorland. The red tractor in the distance, almost like a Dinky toy, was winding round the tortuous twists of the peat road.

"It's not only that," she said quietly. "But ... when you

talk of the Pugh-Smith family as if they were Public Enemy No 1, I feel, well, sad. In your jealousy of them, you look past the good that is in them."

James snorted and lit another cigarette.

"I suppose it's human not to trust people who come from a different culture to ours. Yet, you know, people everywhere are basically the same underneath. We all have a mix of good and bad; we all want to have a sense of self-worth; we all need something to give sense and meaning to our lives."

"Huh! Who needs sense and meaning sorted out when you're rotten with money and puffed up with power?" Quickly James got to his feet and began to fill a sack with the smaller, more crumbly peat. "All this talk setting the world to rights - it doesn't get the work done, does it?"

The tractor driver drove towards them with an accuracy of judgement that allowed for the large boulders on one side and the sticky peat soil on the other. The small group began to throw peats into the trailer with renewed energy while Alan, the driver, alighted to survey the resting position of those big wheels.

"Safe enough, I think. But we'd better not make this load too heavy." And then, as an afterthought, he said, "My old man was waiting for me when I reached with the last load. Never seen him in such a foul temper!"

"What was wrong?" Mrs Maclean asked, not stopping in her rhythmic bend - lift - throw.

"Seems the Estate, Pugh-Smith I mean, has bought the fishing rights for our river."

"He did *what*?" James' voice rose, as if a bolt of pure anger was surging through him.

"You heard. It was on the radio news. Plus some comments about an expected public outcry, this being the only decent river left for the locals to fish on."

"That's *it*." James shouted. "*That is it*." It was almost a cry of exaltation, as if it proved a point. "It's the best fishing river on the island, totally wasted on us natives."

"Come on, we'll talk about it at home," Mrs Maclean said in a soft, coaxing voice. She had been up since six, juggling with the elaborate food preparations involved in this annual ritual of taking home their fuel supply; more food preparation, bordering on the Cordon Bleu, up at the Estate; and now this sheer hard labour. She was tired and wanted to go home.

Later, as they gathered overjackets, spades and picnic things in preparation for their journey home, James took Graham aside.

In an ordinary, everyday voice he said, "They're not going to win. If we can't fish legally, we'll do it without their permission. After all, if there is a God, the fish in the sea and lochs and rivers belong to him, and we never had to ask his permission!"

Graham wasn't sure about the theology that lay behind James' words. He frowned lightly. "Uh, you mean poaching? Don't think my mother would be wildly happy with that idea."

It was a schoolboy's remark, which they both recognized, and James instantly had that jaw-forward look which meets life like a plough.

"Oh, grow up, Graham! Untie those apron strings. I'm sure if your father was alive, he'd understand. Look at you - you've already got the mark of a guy who's spent too much time with his mammy!"

"Sounds like a Kamikaze act to me, that's all," Graham said defensively. "What about the watchers?"

"No problem. You can sniff around and find out - via your mother and that Sheleen girl - when they'll be tied up. You know, doing rounds in other areas, or working with the horses, or whatever ... "

"Uh ... "

"Well?"

"I'll think about it," Graham said to James, without fully meeting his eye. His friend's suggestion sent his mind furtively sliding down into a dark pool of secret knowledge. His mother would know exactly which night the watchers were tied up; she had often inadvertently mentioned the fact.

Swiftly, he yanked the thoughts back onto safer ground. He couldn't, he wouldn't, do such a thing. Or would he?

CHAPTER 5

THE CAUSE OF THE BLUSH

"I'm thankful that's the peats over for another year." Mary Maclean eyed the sink piled high with dirty dishes and took another sip of her tea.

Graham, having just forked a large piece of chilled lemon cheesecake into his mouth, could only mumble in agreement.

"It's not fair," she complained. "You can sit there and devour all those calories and not put on one ounce. All I have to do is look at a cake and the pounds go on!"

"Rubbish! Remember when you tried on your wedding dress - the day you were cleaning out that old chest? It still fitted you, didn't it?"

"Only if I took a deep breath, and didn't breathe out again!" And then, "It bought back a lot of memories, Graham. The dress, the day, your father ... "

"My father. It's funny, I don't remember him for ages, but then, once in a while, something comes back in a wave, the way he ruffled my hair; the sound of his whistling as he walked up the path; his laughter." The memories kept coming, flashing across the screen of his mind. "And plenty of memories on film, even though they're pretty awful photos."

"I always seemed to chop off heads in my photographs," she laughed. "And he would say that the practical side of my brain was seriously underdeveloped! Oh, I missed his teasing for such a long time. You know, before Iain died, I would never have believed that I would feel so ... so incomplete without him. As if half of me had gone."

"Suppose not," Graham said thoughtfully. "But as they say, 'You've come a long way, baby.' He'd be surprised now to see how developed the practical side of your brain is. You're so independent, a real liberated woman."

"Mmmm, I wonder about that. Yes, I wonder. To be independent is good. It can be pretty lonely, too."

Graham was silent. He was thinking how little you could ever really know about another person and that made him uneasy. He changed the subject. "Oh, I almost forgot. Sheleen said to tell you that Samuel Somebody-or-Other is coming tomorrow."

His mother picked up her mug of tea, drank too much, too fast, choked and coughed. "That would be Samuel Stern, her father's accountant." She tried to sound casual, but her face had gone a vivid red.

To Graham, there was something oddly endearing about her blushing. "Hey, you're like the cat who's just swallowed the cream, and been found out!"

"I'm pleased ... " she groped for words, "to hear that he's coming this early on in the summer. I thought he said something about August, that's all."

"And how do you know him so well? You don't usually rub shoulders with your social betters, do you?"

Although his voice held a teasing note, Graham experienced a subtle shift in his own emotions. Who was this Stern guy? What did he mean to his mother?

"He's Mr Pugh-Smith's accountant," she repeated.

"I know that much. Sounds foreign - I mean, the way you pronounce his name. Is he a foreigner?"

"Not really. Unless you consider an Englishman a foreigner! His parents were German, and Jewish." She smiled and the fine lines at the corners of her mouth softened. "Samuel is a Jew who believes that Jesus is the Messiah."

"The - what?"

"The Messiah, the Son of the Living God."

"Oh." He examined the cake crumbs with affected interest. Two desires had collided in his head: The desire to know more about The Cause of the Blush, and the desire not to earn another sermon.

A light knocking at the front door interrupted his reverie. It was Timothy.

"Timothy!" Mrs Maclean welcomed. "Come in, dear. Aha, I think you smelt my lemon cheesecake up there at the Estate, is that right?"

He didn't answer her smile, but blinked hard as though he were on the verge of crying, even though his eyes were dry.

"What's up, small guy?" Graham squatted down low beside him, so that they were on the same level.

"Dad won't let me have Glen's puppy."

"Won't he now?"

"No. He said ... he said it wouldn't be properly trained, that it would make the sheep worried!" He stormed on, almost spitting out the words.

Mrs Maclean laughed, and Timothy shot her an indignant glance.

"Sorry, dear," she said hastily. "I know what you mean. Dogs aren't allowed to worry sheep, are they? They're not allowed to chase them and frighten them."

'Someone should worry that guy,' Graham thought, 'he's not a father, he's a machine.' Aloud he said, "Tell you what. We'll look after the puppy here for you, but he'll be your pup. Yours. You choose his name, you choose where to take him for walks. We'll train him together. Okay, small guy?"

"Okay! Very okay!" Timothy gave a crow of pleasure, sweetly oblivious to Mrs Maclean's lips soundlessly framing the words "Won't work." He then went rocketing

41

ahead to the old barn, bellowing, "Ready or not, here I come!" Graham followed behind at a more leisurely pace.

Inside the barn the dust smelt sweet. In another month the hay bales would be piled high to the roof, but now it was almost empty. Except for Glen's puppy, who sat up, yawned, wagged his tail and practically smiled up at them. He was the original charmer and totally conquered little Timothy by going into a paroxysm of drooling ecstasy.

"He's licking my nose! Look, Graham, look!" Timothy knelt beside the puppy and put his arms around him.

"I think he knows you're choosing him as your very own. He knows he's special." Graham felt a sudden, overwhelming surge of affection for both boy and pup. "And he knows you're special."

"I'll call him, Graham - after you!"

"Help! What will happen then when you shout 'Come to heel, Graham'? We'll both come running!"

"Um, how about Grey, then? He's black and white. Black and white makes grey, doesn't it?"

"Can't argue with that, can I? Look, I've got to play King of the Sink right now. You can play with uh ... Grey for as long as you like."

"Can I? Brill! Oh, Graham, Sheleen asked if you could take her out to the summer house on the moor. The shieling - that's what it's called, isn't it? Remember, you went there for a walk last year and could I go with you ... ? "

Graham smilingly mouthed 'Not a chance!' and left Timothy to the mercy of the pup's lathering tongue.

Once back inside the house, Graham was propelled by his mother to the dishes and the detergent. "See that wee guy? Give him an inch and he'll take a mile. He now wants to walk out to the shieling with Sheleen and I!"

"Oh." His mother wiped the table and placed on it a fresh red and white checked cloth, then arranged a pottery jug of wild flowers in the centre.

He looked at her, puzzled by her lack of reaction. "What do you mean, 'Oh'?"

"Nothing. Nothing at all."

"You like Sheleen, don't you?"

"Of course I do. You couldn't meet a nicer girl than Sheleen," she said evasively, avoiding his questioning eye. And then, "Only, don't think of her in a long-term way, that's all."

"Huh?"

There was a brief, electric silence, punctuated only by the sleepy chirruping of a bird beyond the open window.

At last, his mother spoke. "I overheard a conversation between Sheleen and her mother this morning. They had been riding quite early and were putting the horses in the stable. I was in that small gun room looking for the barbecue stuff and ... "

"And?"

"Her mother was saying something about how good it was that the two of you could so easily pick up the friendship. From where you left off last summer, I think she meant. A friendship like that was good for broadening one's mind - associating with people who had completely different lifestyles.

"Sheleen said, 'What are you getting at, Mum?' and Mrs Pugh-Smith said to remember that it was only a summer friendship. And nothing more. Both of you came from different worlds, she said."

"Did Sheleen say .... anything?"

His mother looked stricken. "She didn't say anything for a while. Then she said, 'That's the icing on the cake - that we both know it'll never be serious.' "

Graham didn't speak. He wanted time to go backwards, just five minutes, to when his mother was arranging the pottery jug on the table.

"Graham?"

"Uh-huh?"

"How do you - feel about that?"

He could not meet her eyes, afraid of what his own might show. Outside the sink window, he could see that the sun was beginning to dip towards the west. The pink light would soon vanish, leaving the fields cold and grey.

"No big deal, Mum," he said. "Forget it." He washed the dishes as thoroughly as he had closed the conversation, and then went outside.

The night was still, but inside him there was turmoil. He couldn't pin a description on his feelings, but felt himself faltering on the edge of some pit. The friendship, the long talking sessions, the verbal boxing matches, the bond of secret, mutual laughter, all were scattered, useless, valueless, behind him.

He walked slowly towards the barn, cold and confused, as the midsummer day slowly died around him.

There were two things he had to do. One was to send Sheleen a message via Timothy, that he'd be too busy to go to the shielings this summer. The other was to phone James. "Time I started living, time I had some adventure," he rehearsed aloud, covering up the cold sadness inside.

CHAPTER 6

THE SIXTH ADVENTURE

By the time they set off on their sixth 'adventure' Graham decided it was all a bore. One big yawn. Thankfully, they could only go out poaching about once a week, when Graham had gleaned enough information from his mother to know that it would be safe.

'Poor Mum, little does she know that she's our informer.' He thought of his recent near-silent treatment of her. Silence was a dreadful kind of lying, he reflected.

All the time, he worked like a slave around the house and croft; painting walls inside and out, fixing fences, mending the roof tiles. He wanted there to be something to say 'It was Graham Maclean's final summer at home, and he made a difference.' At the same time, he wanted to shut Sheleen out of his mind, although it was hard with little Timothy constantly round his feet. So he lived through the hours, the days and the weeks, taking them as they came, knowing they would never come again.

And now here he was once more, carrying the heavy net towards the river. At that point, however, he tripped and sent a startled grouse squabbling skywards.

James swore at him.

Quickly Graham got to his feet and followed James into the last of the twilight glow of the summer evening. The air was now cool and filled with the aroma of heather and wet peat-soil.

"You're a positive little dynamo tonight, aren't you?" James said with heavy sarcasm. "Move it, man."

The usual ripple of instructions sounded in Graham's ear. "Tie the end of the net. Now! Tighter! Right, I'll wade across." Graham mechanically tied the end of the heavy net to a wooden stake driven into the soil and watched James wade across the river, and then tie the net to a stake on the opposite bank.

His thoughts became a slow meaningless procession imaging the net, the salmon, his mother's cooking, his mother, Sheleen ...

Unable to cope with the thought, he covered it up in action. His job was to act as the look-out while James was setting the net, so he walked alongside the river which curled and mumbled its course through the moorland. The seared emptiness of the moors found an echo in his own aloneness.

He walked till he felt a kind of weariness overcoming him. He was tired, right down to the soles of his feet. Tired and cold and numbingly bored. He wished he were somewhere, anywhere, else.

His thoughts, going out of control, slid back towards his mother and her voice, saying 'my prodigal son'. He peered at the date on his watch and registered the fact that it had been over six weeks since she had called him that. Six weeks, it felt like six years ... six hundred years.

'Nothing amongst the pig swill could have been worse than this,' he thought, going back to that old, old story. 'Anyway, the son in that set-up eventually came to himself and went back to the father. I can't go back to my mother and say, "Hey, Mum, forgot to tell you, but I've been using you as an informer against your employer. We're raking in the money at the expense of his salmon. But so what, the salmon's free, isn't it? What Pugh-Smith won't know, won't hurt him. Right? Right, Mum?"'

Shivering, despite his denim jacket and jeans, he jerked back his thoughts with a great effort. "Blow all these crazy thoughts," he muttered to himself. "I'd like to stuff them in the salmon bag and ship them down the river."

Over the last few weeks he had schooled himself not to give in to painful memories. He had had to train himself not to think of Sheleen - In the same way he had trained his hands not to reach for the phone whenever she had sent him a bewildered message, 'Why aren't you coming over? Why are you never in when I call? What's wrong?'

Blocking out the thoughts and avoiding a spot of treacherous, boggy ground, he made his way back to James.

"What kept you?" James said. "I was beginning to think you had spotted the watchers."

"Nothing there."

"Good. Sit down. Time we divided the spoils."

"The what?"

"The money, stupid. Oh, c'mon - don't strain the brain! Honestly, I think I've only got one nerve left tonight, and you're leaning on it." Half amused, half annoyed, he counted out some notes and handed them over to Graham. "That's your share. Not bad, is it?"

"Yes, uh ... no, I mean. Thanks."

"It doesn't give me the same gut-satisfaction as being able to personally rearrange Puke-Smith's face," James said, "but it helps. It helps. What d'you plan to do with it?"

For one sharp moment there was silence.

"Hey, what's with you, man? Wake up, Graham. Look lively, man!" James's voice was light, but as his face turned towards Graham, his eyes were waiting, calculating.

"Just thinking how I'd spend it, that's all. Maybe a bit of gold jewellery for my mother ... " Graham pressed his lips together and made a half-smile. "No, she'd ask too many questions. Suppose I'll need it when I go to College. All students are flat broke, aren't they?"

"I wasn't. Ever." A kind of wan smile flickered across James's face, but he didn't elaborate.

They sat in silence for a long time. Until it was broken by a faint, faraway bang of a vehicle door slamming shut. Faraway, but still too close for comfort.

"What's ... "

"Shhh!" James hissed. Instantly they felt overwhelmed by silence. Total silence. Weighted. Heavy.

James handed Graham the binoculars and gestured towards a nearby hillock.

Swiftly, running in a low crouch, Graham made for a large boulder on the hillock. He trained the binoculars where the sound had come from, his fingers trembling slightly as he thumbed the focusing wheel.

He counted one, two, three watchers with their dogs striding up towards him. They were spaced out from each other by several yards. Graham felt his heart begin to pump at a sickening rate, and his brain seemed to have jammed. In panic, he looked back towards James. *His* brain must have been working, because he took one look at Graham's stricken face, and ran.

Dread rose chokingly in Graham's throat. Where could he run for cover?

The river - if only he could get down to the river. Further downstream, there were plenty of big boulders to hide behind. Silently, swiftly, he ran over the uneven moorland, skipping over the more boggy ground.

Just as he was beginning to gather up speed, his feet were suddenly sucked from under him, and he was floundering in the embracing soil. It was cold, with a terrible, purposeful drag to it. As he sank to his knees he felt an odd little thrill of fear.

'Oh God ... Oh God, help me!' The words yelled in his mind, but no sound came from him.

Swaying sideways, his eyes fixed on a clump of heather jutting over the peat bog. Gasping, his arms outstretched, he managed to grab hold of it and flung the top half of his body flat over the sticky soil.

The mud was thigh-high on his jeans when he dragged himself onto the firmer, heather-covered soil. For a short moment he lay there, his breath coming in a series of heaving gasps, staring mute and exhausted into the midnight sky. It was darker now, but never completely dark at this time of year.

The sound of dogs barking reminded him of the merciless truth - he was still the quarry. He got up and started to run. It took all he had to reach the river. Without looking round, he stepped into it.

A band of ice seemed to grip one ankle. Then the other. Unbelievable that the water would be so cold in the height of summer! When he had waded towards the far side of the river where the water only came up to his knees, he took up a squatting position. Two big river boulders gave him cover.

The cold! He could hardly stand it - but what was the alternative? Fear began to rise within him, pushing its way up from his stomach, and into his throat with a cold, choking pressure. He swallowed, twice.

He could hear the sound of voices, coming nearer at first, and then receding. He didn't move. Neither did he spare a thought for the net which would surely be confiscated.

"Come on, go! Go!" he willed, clenching his teeth and whispering into the leaden boulders. And it was hard to be sure if they had finally gone, because of the noise the river made. It seemed much louder than it had done about half an hour ago - as though the whole night was made up of the noise of troubled, restless water.

"Must be well after midnight now," he whispered to himself. He visualized his mother, relaxed and cosied up in bed. He had mentioned to her that he might be late in coming home; "Going for a real long walk" was his parting explanation.

Again the image of the prodigal son came to his mind - he could picture it; clearly and sharply as a camera must see things happen. First of all, a 'snapshot' of the son's hand in the pigswill. Then, one of the same hands - but this time clean- as the father slipped on the ring of love, the token of sonship.

"The cold is making my brain mushy," he groaned silently. He found a bit of self-mockery helped. It pushed the unreal, the unbelievable, weight of anxiety away, until finally he was sure the watchers were away.

He waded soundlessly out of the river. Dazed, thoroughly numb and yet trembling all over, he made his way home. As he crossed an old wooden bridge leading to his village, a figure loomed out in front of him.

It was James.

"Those pigs! They've stolen my net ... " His voice drifted off into a hostile silence.

"Aw, who cares - "

"'Who cares?' What d'you mean? I care!"

"Well, get this," Graham said, matching anger to anger. "I don't give a flying leap about your stupid net."

James stood still and concentrated his whole attention on this stranger who was Graham Maclean. "You were scared silly - is that it? I didn't know you were chicken!"

"I'm soaked, frozen - sick fed up!" Graham said, snarling like a bad guy in the Westerns. "Take your filthy money. Here!" With that, he bundled the ten-pound notes towards James. The notes weren't so much filthy, as sopping wet.

James glared at him, his face a mask of scorn and anger. "Right, Mammy's boy - listen to this and listen good! If you ever feel like playing Supergrass about tonight, or the other nights - spare a thought for your precious mother. I doubt if they'll ever be able to pin the poaching on us, but if they do, or if you spill the beans, I'll just say *she* gave us all the information we needed. And, good little Christian that she is, she won't be able to deny it. Get it?"

"If there's one thing I don't need right now, it's a far-out scene like this. I'm off." Graham's voice was cold and final. James heard it and said nothing.

Graham strode away without a backward glance, wanting to put a quick million miles between himself and the river. Between himself and James. And, more than that, between himself and those thoughts that still plagued him.

"Someone Up There heard me when I was being sucked into that bog," he concluded, watching the clouds straying across the darkening sky. And all the time he was marching homeward, he could hear a refrain in his mind, "There is a God! There is a God!"

CHAPTER 7

THE CAUSE OF THE BLUSH APPEARS

"They didn't catch the poachers last night, then?"

"No, Mary. They saw the figure of one running away towards the hills. Big Duncan gave chase for a moment, but he's not exactly in the Olympics league, and he soon lost sight of him."

Graham listened to the conversation between his mother and The Cause of the Blush, who had dropped in for a cup of coffee. If you could call staying for two hours 'dropping in'.

No, that wasn't fair, Graham thought. Another time, he would have found this man interesting. Darkly handsome, fortyish, with a dry sense of humour, Samuel Stern was thoroughly likeable. But Graham felt too chewed up this evening for ordinary feelings such as liking.

"Strange, wasn't it, that the dogs seemed to follow a scent along the river bank?" Samuel said thoughtfully. "There was no one there. I think Jerram was a bit disappointed with his dogs!"

Mary Maclean seemed to be on the brink of saying something but instead walked over to the window, open to the early evening breeze. Summer poured into the house with the faint sweetness of newly cut grass, and the plaintive notes of bird song trembled in the air and melted softly away into the calm of the sleepy day.

Her cameo face was thoughtful as she eventually said, "I suppose ... I suppose it's wrong say this, but you see, I can understand how they feel. The poachers, I mean. Every good river in the area used only by wealthy outsiders. Not by the people who work the land; whose fathers worked the land; whose forefathers worked the land - but by total strangers. It doesn't seem fair."

A bout of coughing from Graham interrupted her train of thought. "Graham, *where* did you get such a bad cold? You woke me up with your non-stop sneezing last night! Look, I'll make you another hot drink."

"Don't fuss, Mum! I'll have to survive coughs and colds and sneezes when I go to live on the mainland. I'll look after myself, okay?"

"That's right, Graham. Strike a blow for Men's Liberation," Samuel Stern said, a little smile hovering around his mouth.

"Talking of Liberation, Graham," Mrs Maclean laughed, "when I saw your jeans washed and hung out on the line this morning - it gave me hope. I thought I'd need to enrol you in some de-programming course, to rid you of those male chauvinistic traits. Especially before you were let loose in some Hall of Residence!"

"I'm shocked, Mary!" Samuel teased. "How could you be so hard on your only son?"

"Practice, Samuel. Practice ... Oh, look at the time! I have to run over to the Manse with this baking for the Youth Fellowship. Make Samuel another cup of coffee, Graham."

"Your mother doesn't want me to have caffeine withdrawal symptoms in front of you, Graham. And a whole half hour has gone by since I've had a cup!" Samuel laughed his rich, deep burst of laughter and fine lines sprayed out from around his dark eyes.

As Graham busied himself making coffee, he listened to their voices making everyday, ordinary conversation and a core of loneliness twisted inside him. Not of jealousy for the closeness his mother and Samuel seemed to share, but how uncomplicated their lives seemed to be. He envied them.

"One cup of coffee coming up," he said aloud, handing Samuel a cup and flopping down in a chair opposite him.

After Mrs Maclean left, armed with her famous spicy apple teacake, Graham and Samuel Stern chatted about dogs and crops and accountancy.

Slowly, in the gathering twilight, Graham felt the ordinary world setting comfortably into place around him. The hills in the west were touched with pink from the last rays of the setting sun as he got up to make yet another cup of coffee.

"Tell me, Graham," Samuel said as he accepted the coffee cup, "why do you dislike the Pugh-Smiths so much?" The question was so unexpected, and the eyes so intense, that it gave Graham a feeling of having been caught and pinned in place by a physical force.

"Uh ... how do you mean?" Hearing the defensive tone of his own voice Graham bit back the words, 'None of your business, anyway!' Instead he forced himself to hold his emotions in check and listened to what Samuel had to say.

"Timothy and Sheleen - I think they're disappointed that you don't come over to the Estate any more. Like you did last summer."

"It's different for me this year, though. I *see* things differently. The whole set-up makes me snarl inside - if they'd just get off that power trip they're on ... "

The words tumbled out because there was a quality in the older man's listening which drew out everything he wanted to say.

When the verbal storm was over, Samuel's eyes met his. There was a tiny silence in which the noise of the open fire sounded oddly loud.

"You really, you only mean Jerram Pugh-Smith, don't you? The rest of them; Sheleen, Timothy, their mother, are kind and warm. But Graham, it's a hard thing to learn warmth. You have to grow up feeling it, you know, and Jerram, he never did. Nobody had given that feeling to him."

"Not his mother, anyway."

"No. And it's difficult for him to learn a different way to be. Now, if he knew the Lord ... "

Graham had a frantic sense of not wanting to hear the rest, yet he found himself asking, "How come ... you being a Jew ... how come you believe in - in all that?"

"Have you got all night?" Samuel smiled and the whole humour and vivid intelligence and strength of the man's face made Graham recognize again why his mother liked him so much.

"Now, don't panic Graham, I'll make it brief. I was born a Jew, I enjoyed being a Jew; the Jewish holidays and festivals were so central to my life, Rosh Hashannah, Yom Kippur, the Passover - you'll know all about that one! - and Channukah. And the food. Jewish food is wonderful. Your mother wants to learn some of the traditional recipes! But the religious part of being a Jew, well, it never figured much in my life, I'm afraid. As for the name Jesus Christ, I only knew it as a swear word ...

"About five years ago, a German accountant came to work at our firm. I couldn't stand the man! Not because of what the Germans did to my grandparents in Dachau, no - he was such a cold and calculating sort of fellow. A bit like Jerram Pugh-Smith."

Samuel turned the coffee cup round in his hands as he continued. "He had to do a two-year stint at our office in the States, in Boston. And I didn't miss him one bit in that time! But when he came back he was so different, it was unbelievable."

"In what way?" Graham asked.

"In every way. Manner, appearance - I mean, he even *looked* different. His eyes struck me the very first day he came back; no longer cold and disinterested, but warm and alive and ... sort of caring. And so he was. I could only think of the caterpillar turning into a butterfly."

Graham got up and switched on the lamp beside him. The light hardly made any difference to the room at first. It had to compete with some remnants of daylight still stealing in from the window.

"Anyway, to cut a long story short, I began to avoid him like a plague when I found out he was one of those 'born again' folk. Even though he never once tried to preach at me. But when I saw how he reacted to various things that went wrong with his life - I'm telling you, I *had* to notice. A servant of God was in my life, just like your mother is in yours, Graham."

Graham didn't reply and Samuel continued.

"I remember cornering him one day about this Jesus. We talked a lot and his parting shot was 'Either Jesus never was or he still is - I challenge you to find out for yourself!' "

"And I did, through the Bible. Even in the Old Testament - especially Isaiah 53 and other chapters - Jesus was there. I was captivated and conquered by this Jesus, my Messiah. I didn't have to commit intellectual suicide to become a believer in Jesus. This God, this Jesus, may be known. He is a Someone - "

"And guess what? You stopped using his name as a swear word!" Graham interrupted.

"That's right! In fact, that's how I knew, one day, that this is what I wanted. Somebody swore using his name, and it hurt me so much, it was like a physical pain. Can you understand that, Graham?"

"Can't understand anything of it, full stop!" Graham said, with a catch in his voice which was supposed to pass for laughter. "If there is a God, I don't suppose he is interested in me."

"That's where you're wrong, Graham. God is not just a Superpower, the Great Computer in the Skies. He cares for you, he sent his only Son to die for you. That is all part of his plan."

"Look, you have your belief - I have mine. I just 'happen' to be here on this planet, and there's no plan behind it, at least that I can see."

As Graham spoke, he knew he was shifting onto different ground. Yet still through the excuses and side-tracking forming in his mind came a stab of the old nightmare fear - what if he himself was wrong all along?

What about last night's instinctive reaction when he was almost swallowed up by the boggy ground?

"Doesn't your conscience tell you that there must be more to life than the here and now?" Samuel asked. He spoke softly, quietly. "You see, Graham, we have been made by another, for another. We have not been made for ourselves, but for him - God." When Samuel saw that Graham was at a loss for words, he went on talking.

"Graham, do you know ... can you understand ... what it means to someone who sees that he is eternally lost to be told that there is hope after all? Hope because of what happened on Christ's cross?"

The words hung between them, stark in the frail evening light. A knock on the door broke through the silence and Graham got up to answer it.

It was Sheleen, and Samuel Stern, sensing the strained atmosphere, excused himself.

They stood in uncomfortable silence after he left. Then they both spoke at once.

"Hi. "

"Hello. "

"How are you?"

"How're you doing?"

"Fine, thank you."

"I'm okay."

After the initial crossed questions-and-answers, Graham asked her in and they both sat down. They chatted, but there remained the awkwardness between them that comes over two people who have once been close but are no longer sure what to say to one another.

"So Timothy still has fishing on the brain? He wants to go out tomorrow?" Graham tried to keep his voice light, suited to the conversation. 'Unpanic,' he told himself. 'Don't get uptight ... play it mellow and easy.'

"Yes. He's had a vomiting bug the last few days, that's why he hasn't been up to see his puppy. But he's red-hot determined to be alright for tomorrow! You know what he's like, stubborn as a mule."

The conversation was light and ordinary, but as Graham looked at those green eyes that he knew so well, that had seen her through so many situations they had shared - those eyes looked troubled.

"Graham?" Sheleen spoke his name with an odd, almost broken note in her voice.

"Yes?"

"Can I ask you something?"

"Sure. Fire away."

"Can you ... can you look at me straight in the face and say that last summer doesn't mean anything to you now? And all these other summers? Can you ... say that?"

The question was so unexpected, so far removed from the previous conversation that he was unprepared. He would have liked, just then, to lift his hand and stroke her hair, but he stopped himself. A kind of pain closed in on him as he looked back on these other summers and saw, really saw, what good times they had enjoyed together.

At that moment, his mother stepped into the house, and the moment passed. Whatever he might have found to say, it was too late.

CHAPTER 8

A TESTING TIME

Timothy's voice, piping loud as he pummelled Graham with questions, frightened away any fish within a five-mile radius.

"Shhh! Don't try to be more of a loudmouth than nature already made you," Graham teased as he watched the little boy cracking his fishing line like a lion-tamers whip.

"I'm not a loudmouth!"

"No? Only a machine-gun, then. You go pow-pow-pow! Only it's not bullets that come out, it's words!"

Timothy flashed a gap-toothed grin and cast again, even more wildly, into the looking glass that was the loch. The nearby hills were reflected there in a patchwork of colour, revealing a hidden world with a slow heartbeat. A world of silence, serenity and incredible beauty. Above the loch, a pheasant launched into her flight through the empty bright afternoon.

"Nearly got that one!" Timothy crowed triumphantly.

"Say that again."

"Nearly got that fish, Graham."

"That makes ten times you've said that in the last five minutes." Graham grinned, then added, "So all your family's away at the Agricultural Show? Thought you'd like to be there, Timothy. See the tractors and the other machinery."

"I'd rather go fishing with you! Anyway, Mum said I would get too tired at the Show after being sick the last few days. I didn't tell her I was sick again this morning, or she wouldn't have let me go anywhere!"

"Sick again? You are a bit of a paleface today, now that you mention it. Oh boy, your mum will read you the riot act if you're sick out here."

"I won't! I won't - I promise!"

The 'promise' was not kept, for, about an hour later, Timothy threw up over the big flat stone he was standing on. It was not a large amount, but as Graham glanced at it, he stopped and stared more closely. What was that spot of dark stuff? It looked almost like blood. Surely not.

He looked at Timothy, now sitting down and breathing hard, and noticed the ashen face and the cold, clammy skin. This was one sick little boy.

The fish forgotten, the fishing tackle left behind, Graham lifted Timothy onto his back and started walking. He plunged through the springy purple heather with quick, nervous strides. There was no sound at all, now that the little boy had quietened. The silence wrapped around them like a blanket, the sculptured clouds quietly drifted in the depthless sky, the shadows on the hills changed their mysterious shape. For Graham, it was not an empty silence, but one charged with responsibility and anxiety.

He decided to head for the doctor's surgery, which was nearer than the Lodge. In any case, Timothy's family were away on the other side of the island and there was no way of contacting them. Fortunately, old Dr. Jones was at the surgery when they eventually reached and didn't mind being disturbed.

He examined the boy, and did a routine test of the sample Graham had scooped into the bait drum.

"I think we'll run this little fellow to hospital and get them to do a few tests. As for his parents, I'm sure the best thing to do is to leave word with the Lodge."

Under the grey cliff of his eyebrows, the doctor's eyes were troubled.

The sun had almost gone and its last light sloped in a low bright shaft across the children's ward. Some dust motes, having escaped the daily dousing of disinfectants, swirled in the light. And here in the small side room where Timothy was sleeping, there was silence and twilight, and the smell of cleanness and antiseptics.

Time seemed to expand and contract insanely. Even

though the little boy was soundly asleep, Graham continued to hold his hand, and from his compassion there flowered such a vast, incommunicable love to this little heaped form under the duvet. He had been so brave and trusting during the procedures the medical staff had carried out, and when it was all over, he was pathetically glad to slip into bed. 'Timothy, you're a champion!' Graham saluted him silently, and wished, for the hundredth time, that the Pugh-Smiths would come.

As he bent down close to Timothy, and flicked the lock of fair hair away from his forehead, the Pugh-Smith family arrived. There were frantic questions from Jerram Pugh-Smith, while his wife said nothing and leaked tears. Sheleen had that vague, unfocused look of someone moving through a dream.

A doctor appeared and took Leanda and Jerram Pugh-Smith into a small office. Graham sat in silence with Sheleen, and listened to the loud tick of the ward clock. His brain pulsed with the sound, unable now to cope with thought.

He looked up and met Sheleen's eyes, the dread in them was almost palpable. Forgetting the cold facade he had adopted the day before, he hugged her long and hard, murmuring into her hair, "It's okay. He'll be okay."

One glimpse of Jerram Pugh-Smith's face as he approached, broke the silence. It was clear that he hadn't been given reassuring news. Timothy was to be flown by ambulance plane to the mainland, first thing in the morning, he told them. His haemoglobin was low - that meant he was anaemic - and the doctors felt that his condition could be investigated more thoroughly in the children's hospital in Glasgow.

"Could it be l-leukaemia?" Sheleen asked, forcing the words out. She wiped her eyes with the back of one hand, the other clenched into a hard fist. "Could it?"

"Leukaemia?" Her father, whose head was lowered on his hands, now looked up. "No, they did ask about bruising and nose-bleeds and if he'd been feeling under the weather for some time, but we said no, none of these things. Apart from the vomiting bug. And there's no way of knowing if that involved blood, so -"

"Oh no! Not that!" Leanda Pugh-Smith moaned in a wobbly voice. Graham tried not to look at her. He couldn't look the possibility in the eye, either.

"Mum, I'm sorry! I'm so tired I'm not even thinking straight," Sheleen said, annoyed with herself. "It's just that there's this girl in our school and she had to have a bone marrow transplant but she's fine now and anyway it might not be that." The words kept falling and falling until Jerram Pugh-Smith cut her off.

"We're all stupid with this tiredness, Sheleen. The doctors don't know, so we don't know. So there's no point speculating, is there?"

Graham watched helplessly as the family fell apart.

The uncertainty of it all seemed to strike a mortal blow to the basic structure of their lives, leaving them floundering helplessly. He wished that his mother was here - she'd know what to say.

"You know, when we were driving here ... " Mrs Pugh-Smith began in a flat, tired voice, "I saw my face in the wing mirror of the car, and I wanted to throw up. What a woman! What a *mother*! Never around when her son needs her. I never even saw his ... his vomit. Not once. But, oh yes, I praised him when he made it to the toilet and didn't mess on the carpet."

"At least, you were sympathetic, Leanda. When he piped out this morning that he was too tired to go to the Show, and wanted to go fishing with Graham ... well, you know how I went on. How we should do things together as a family. What a joke! We've never allowed ourselves to be a family, have we?"

Jerram Pugh-Smith's voice rose sharply as he continued: "In our family, we're all on our own - each man an island. Look at us, Leanda, permanently buzzing about in a frenzied hurry. As individuals, we all walk in a ... a kind of isolation, completely encased in some invisible plastic bubble."

"Dad!" Sheleen pleaded, "You're right, but we're here now, and we'll do everything in our power to help Timothy. It could have been a lot worse... " Her voice faltered for a second, "but at least, Graham was with him."

At this, Timothy's parents thanked Graham profusely, while he tried to put a name on the feelings this aroused in him. Could it be shame? he wondered.

After a while, Mr Pugh-Smith slipped out into the hospital corridor for a cigarette. Graham followed, trying to pluck up courage to speak to him.

The seconds ticked by and then, with despairing quietness, he cleared his throat and said, "Mr Pugh-Smith ... uh ... I don't know how to say this, but you wouldn't be heaping on the praise if you knew what I'd done. I guess this isn't the time or place to try to ease a guilty conscience, but - I've been poaching at the Estate."

The words came out in a rush. Then he caught his breath, waiting for a reaction, and stared out of the window at the sky above the hospital.

The sunset had dribbled away leaving the sky a leaden grey, that kind of grey that deepens and darkens the greens of shrubbery and trees. Oblongs of fluorescent light fell from the hospital across the uncertain light of the car park. A chorus of birds were doing overtime in a nearby tree.

There was still no reply and Graham continued, his voice loud in his own ears. "I didn't take any money for it. It was just for ... " What *had* it been for, he thought. Adventure, revenge, jealousy?

"Ah yes, the confiscated net." Mr Pugh-Smith shifted, to look directly into Graham's eyes. "And I suppose you're telling me because you feel guilty and a bit ashamed. Well, Graham, maybe now you'll have a better understanding of how I feel tonight."

Graham wanted to turn away. The pain in the older man's eyes was so deep that he wished he hadn't started the conversation.

"It's only right that you should have been with my son through all this. You're more of a father to him than I've ever been. You're the one who takes him fishing and teaches how to train that assorted-breed puppy and listens to his endless chatter. And you made him that go-kart last summer, remember? 'Unsafe!' we shouted when he took a tumble off it one day. And next day it was firewood. No, you haven't forgotten that, have you? Neither did he."

The tone of his voice left no room for argument. "Graham, what have I shared with him? Nothing. Tell me the truth, did Timothy ask for me tonight? Did he?"

"I suppose he didn't have to, really. I told him you'd all be along soon."

"You see? My son doesn't even need me. It was only right that you should be the one who held his hand and talked him through all those tests they did today. The doctor said it made all the difference for Timothy to have his friend there. He trusted you, Graham, and he stayed quite calm.

"My son is the original poor little rich boy, isn't he?"

The raw fury of grief was in his voice as he continued, "Look at you, Graham - your mother took time to share her faith with you. To give you something that's solid and lasting, that doesn't depend on pound notes and power. She taught you to pray, didn't she? I wouldn't even know how to start!"

'If only you knew,' Graham thought, with a fierceness of longing, 'that I'm still in that far-off country, just like the prodigal son. And I don't even know how to start back.'

CHAPTER 9

THE DRAGON'S TEARS

That evening, in the hospital, everything seemed to be happening in slow motion. While Graham and Timothy's family hung around the children's ward, life had seemed to be stopped in a 'hold' position, like a frame of a broken film reel. Then, in the morning, it was as if the 'fast-forward' button was pushed and it was all activity; ambulance plane, a string of instructions from Mrs Pugh-Smith, Senior, to her departing son and daughter-in-law, tears from Sheleen and a last bright wave from Timothy.

"It seems like a week since Timothy was flown away," commented Mrs Maclean to Graham one evening as they washed the dinner dishes, "and yet its only been two days." Then she flashed a teasing, sidelong glance at her son. "Mind you, since you and Sheleen have spent every waking moment together, maybe you didn't feel the time exactly drag ... "

"Now, now, I'm duty-bound to do something to keep Sheleen out of the old dragon's way."

"By that complimentary phrase I take it you mean Mrs Pugh-Smith, Senior."

"Right. She seems to resent the fact that it's Timothy who's ill, not Sheleen. Then she makes such a major production of being Timothy's grandmother - no word of Sheleen."

"Your heart doesn't exactly bleed for the poor old soul, does it? Anyway, Timothy is the important one in all this. He's had no further sickness, and they should have the results of the endoscopy tonight."

"It's only then we'll know for sure if it's leukaemia or not. Sheleen is so desperate to do something to help Timothy - you know, she's even said that she'd be the donor if he needed a bone marrow transplant!"

"But I thought that had been ruled out," flashed Mrs Maclean. "Didn't the blood tests show that his white cell count wasn't all that high? And it has to be very, very high for leukaemia, or so I'm told."

"Oh, I see. Guess that didn't connect up for Sheleen, then."

Mary Maclean finished washing the dishes with a quick, nervous hand, and chatted constantly. Then a smile reached the corners of her mouth in a hesitant little curl. "Graham, before you go down to the Lodge - there's something I'd like you to know."

"Go on, surprise me."

"Samuel has asked me to be his wife."

"Try that in my good ear, Mum. I think I misheard you."

"You heard right first time, Graham! Samuel is taking on a partnership in a firm in town and he hopes to move up in a month or two and ... Well, go on, what do you think?"

"Best news I've heard for ages," Graham said, his voice sure, his bear-hug enthusiastic. "You're a real good judge of character, Mum. Samuel Stern is so right for you in every way, but," he added, throwing her a devilish grin, "can he cut peats?"

"So I should test him out on the peat iron before I say 'I do'?" She gave herself over to laughter. "Mmmm, think of it, Samuel and peats. We wouldn't just be talking slow there, we'd be talking tortoise!"

Then she added, "The house is in your name, love, but we'll live here for a while after ... if that's all right with you."

It was, but before he could reply, the telephone rang and Mrs Maclean went to answer it. The conversation seemed short, sharp and to the point.

"You're wanted down at the Lodge straight away. Graham," she said, putting down the receiver.

"Oh, it was Sheleen, then? You should have let ... "

"It was her grandmother, actually, and she didn't sound her usual ice-maiden self. I hope Timothy isn't any worse."

The sky was changing into its early evening colours as

Graham left the house; the blue was dying, and giving way to flushes of hot pink and orange and indigo. The hills stretching to the west were an unbelievable misty mauvish colour. The evening was full of reflected light and the gentle movement of sheep and birds.

"Perhaps tonight ... if it's good news about Timothy ..." he thought, soaking in the spacious solitude all around him, "perhaps I could ask Sheleen to explain that remark about the 'icing on the cake' - does she still feel that way? That I'm some sort of entertainment to while away the summer? But ... surely not! And if she does honestly feel that way - what then?" He sighed, wondering how a person can creep in another's brain, and never leave them alone.

At the Lodge, Mrs Pugh-Smith, Senior, was sitting in the plush lounge, obviously expecting him.

"Any news of Timothy?" Graham asked by way of greeting.

"It's good news, I'm pleased to say. Leukaemia is definitely ruled out, but the endo... endoc ... " (Graham felt an odd little pleasure in her inability to pronounce the word) "...the test showed that the bleeding was caused by a small tear in the stomach lining."

"How on earth - "

"They don't know. Something he swallowed by accident, perhaps - who knows? In any case, it's already showing signs of healing and he'll be home in a couple of days. Naturally, he'll need iron supplements and a nourishing diet and plenty of rest."

"Thank God," Graham said, and there was an unexpected catch in his voice. He cared for the wee guy more than he wanted to admit and badgered her for more information. Eventually the questions-and-answers drizzled and stopped and silence fell.

What was going on? he thought. There was something pretty intense about the old dragon tonight. Her eyes were watchful, and yet, oddly, at the same time had a kind of glazed look that made Graham feel she didn't really see him at all. At times she seemed so remote that she was almost not there. Strange, considering the *bigness* of the good news.

The ringing of the telephone cut through the roaring silence.

"That'll be for you, Graham," Mrs Pugh-Smith said in a voice that was all at once mechanical and tight and wary.

It was indeed for him, and the caller was the younger Mrs Pugh-Smith. They talked about Timothy for a few moments and then he was asked, "Has she told you yet - about Sheleen?"

He felt a rush of cold prickling over his skin as she went on.

Sheleen had taken off somewhere in the afternoon - she wanted time to be alone. Could he, Graham, find her? - her grandmother thought she had gone the moorland way. Could she have gone to the shielings? Could he go and look?

His fingers twisting and re-twisting the telephone cord, Graham tried to reassure her. At least, when he could get a word in edgeways. After three attempts at "Yes, but why?" he managed to say, "Look, I don't understand. You're saying Sheleen took off as soon as she knew Timothy was okay?"

"Yes, you see, only minutes before then, her grandmother had let slip some pretty devastating information." The words coming through the receiver were now only a whisper of sound, and Graham could hear Mrs Pugh-Smith's breath coming out in a long quivering sigh.

"She told Sheleen that ... that she wasn't Timothy's sister. That she wasn't our child. That she was adopted."

"She's what?"

"Adopted."

"But, that's not true, surely?"

"It's difficult to explain over the phone, Graham. We - Jerram and I - wanted a family early on in our married life. But it wasn't to be, and after, oh six years or so, we adopted a baby girl, Sheleen. Then, as sometimes happens, we eventually had two children of our own."

"For Pete's sake, what a thing for her to hear! What a way to hear. She must feel a total, leftover nothing now!" Graham rubbed the stubble on his face in fierce frustration. Now it was Sheleen Somebody-or-Other, Sheleen

Dot-Dot-Dot, Origins Unknown. "I just can't believe I'm hearing this!" he said aloud.

"I know, I know. Oh, we were going to tell her this summer, before she started Uni," Mrs Pugh-Smith explained. The words broke from her, wrenched deep from some area of distress. "I didn't want her to find out from anyone else - and definitely not now, when we're apart. Oh, Graham, I feel so far away ... please, please go and find her."

"Sure, but - "

"Sheleen hasn't run away. I know that. I know she wouldn't want to worry us, after going through all that with Timothy. But I also know she'll be devastated. And I'm not there to explain, to be with her when she needs someone ... Oh, Graham, go to her! Tell her she's as much my daughter as Timothy and Charles are my sons. It's never been any other way."

Jerram Pugh-Smith's voice came over the phone. There was no trace of patronage in his voice now. "Graham? Graham, go to her. Help her. Make her feel warm and safe and cherished. Besides us, Sheleen cares for you more than anyone else in her world, but you know that, don't you? Do something for me, Graham. Tell her that I'll never, never forget that day she was placed in my arms and I said, 'Hello, daughter'. I bonded with her instantly. Funny, isn't it - fatherly isn't a title that would fit me, and I don't deserve it. So tell her, Graham. And ... "

"Yes?"

"Ask your mother to pray for us. I'm growing frightened for my family. Timothy's illness ... and now this. We're never around when our children need us, and when something does happen, we've nothing to lean on; each crisis makes us come unglued and we fall apart."

The note of quiet desperation in his voice reminded Graham of something, hovering just beyond the grasp of memory - something painful. Oh yes, that day at the beginning of summer when he confronted Mr Pugh-Smith, that memory of desperation. But now that the tables were turned, he could feel no triumph.

Instead, he reassured the voice at the other end of the line and put down the phone. Then he whirled furiously on Mrs Pugh-Smith, Senior, choosing to forget anything he had ever been told about his 'elders and betters'. It was almost a relief to have some clear object to rage against.

"What made you go and say a crazy thing like that to Sheleen? You must have known she'd come completely unstuck - huh? How could you?"

"It just - slipped out. I was so anxious about little Timothy and Sheleen was prattling on about wanting to be the bone marrow donor, if he needed a transplant. I said something like. 'That's a bit unrealistic, considering you're not even a blood relation.' "

Graham felt murderous, but, seeing a suggestion of moisture around the old eyes, put his judgements on hold.

She continued, "And then she made me tell her every-thing. When her parents phoned with the news about Timothy she chatted normally to them, and then left. I had to phone Glasgow, and let her parents know. They were very distressed."

"That kind of thing is bad news," Graham said aloud, letting his mind drift back in time. He remembered his own comments last year, how totally different Sheleen was in appearance compared with the rest of the family. And then, Sheleen's awareness of her grandmother's coldness. Yes, losing your sense of identity was bound to be bad news.

He'd have to call at his house and tell his mother, sling a few things in the haversack, and make for the shieling before the evening wove into night. Before he reached the door, Mrs Pugh-Smith's voice called to him.

"Graham?"

"Yes?"

"I'm sorry. Truly I am."

CHAPTER 10

NO MISTY PATCHES

As Graham left his own home, warmly dressed and with a haversack on his back, he took in a big lungful of night air. Thy sky was now a darkish indigo, with little slivers of gold and pink still showing. A light gauzy mist lay on everything, pearling the grass, drifting over the rippling silk of the nearby loch, and swirling and eddying over the moors.

A chill of fear stirred in his heart as he thought of Sheleen. Would she find the shieling before the night set in? Would she remember to follow the river? What if she go lost? There was absolutely nowhere to shelter till the shieling area was reached, about four miles to the south. And did she have warm clothing on? Perhaps, he thought, you could just as easily die of exposure on a damp summer night as in the depths of winter.

He skirted the edge of the loch, and headed towards the river. All the time, the mist was thickening rapidly and for one heart-stopping moment Graham thought he was lost. Straining to hear any sound that might guide him, he felt as if he had only two ears, and nothing else. He felt as if he consisted solely of two big ears, with no other parts of his body functioning. Then he heard the sound of the river, and he made towards it till the sound became deafening, filling the night.

Following close to the river, he made slow progress, tripping over the occasional stone, fumbling and stumbling his way through the heather.

He rehearsed the words of comfort he had for Sheleen, but, on the other hand, maybe she would rather his quiet nearness. But, supposing she was totally devastated, what would he say?

A kind of despair gripped him as he felt his own inability to help anyone; he felt frightened at the emptiness inside him. He had nothing to offer. No pat answers. After all, when it came to his own life, it felt as adrift as being out in the mist. How could he help anyone?

For about an hour he floundered on through the frail light and the cobwebby-white mist. His legs ached as he walked mile after empty mile, and he wished he didn't have so much time to think. The silence and solitude was tearing at his nerves; for all he knew, he might be the only person left on the planet. His thoughts whirled among bits of ideas and information that crowded into his mind and blew about there. Imagination didn't do any good, either, he thought as his mind flicked back to Sheleen, then James, then his mother and Samuel Stern.

Finally, he allowed his brain to settle on Timothy. Timothy with the puppy; running, chasing, hooting with that kind of laughter that took over his whole body until both he and the puppy would get entangled and fall in a heap onto the ground. Timothy, who loved to tickle and wrestle and never asked you to stop. "Thank God that he's okay," he murmured.

At that moment, through the tendrils of mist, he saw a stone wall looming up in front of him. A ruined shieling. And then another, and another. And there it was, his father's shieling, which he and James had renovated and made habitable a few summers ago.

Shaped almost like an igloo, it was built wholly of stone with a turf roof. It had housed his grandparents over many summers, before World War II, and it was they who had given it the Gaelic name of Airigh Fad-As, The Distant Shieling.

Beside the building was another renovated shieling which belonged to James' family. Knowing that both buildings were never locked, he gingerly opened the wooden door of Airigh Fad-As.

Huddled in a corner inside the cold, dark building was Sheleen. Her face was shadowy, unknowable.

"Hi, Sheleen," he said awkwardly, as he let the haversack slip onto the ground. "Glad you found your way here. This mist is only good for ghosts and spooks!"

"Did my grandmother send you out looking for me?" she asked. "I really wanted to be alone, Graham - she knew I wasn't running away."

He felt hurt, but made a business of lighting a fire with the firelighters and firewood from his haversack. At first, the firelight seemed little more than an impertinent gleam, the smallest slug of life, but then its light became yellow and white and leaping, dividing the inside of the old stone building into shadow and light.

"I think there's peat in a sack over here, left over from last year ... That's it." He arranged the peats over the firewood and tried to channel the conversation into the direction of Timothy's recovery.

All the time, his heart ached for Sheleen, and her stiff politeness, and also for his own inability to comfort her. He suspected the calmness was only a temporary reaction, a protective device she had wrapped herself in, a screen to ward off those desolate thoughts.

"You know, when I was about ten," he said, as he sat back on his heels and stared into the fire. "I used to fantasise about being adopted, and I'd daydream that your folk were my true parents. Then I'd feel so guilty when I'd look at my mother!"

She didn't reply, instead turned her head so that she was a black, faceless block of shadow.

And Graham realized that it was sheer crying stupidity to compare his fantasy with her reality. Undaunted, he continued to rattle on to fill out the silence. Word for word, he relayed her parents message, and then his mother's parting words when he had left home.

"Say that again, Graham."

"What?"

"What your mother said."

"About your self-identity, you mean? Can't remember exactly, but something like - if you belonged to the Lord, there would be no identity crisis in your life. You'd know who you were, and whose you were. You'd know what gave your life meaning, you'd know where you were going. I suppose she meant that there would be no misty patches in your life!"

He reached out for her and could not find her hand. Her calm was unnerving to him because it was so unnatural.

"What else did she say?" she asked.

"Hold on till I think ... Oh yes, something about God loving his own people from all eternity. And when one of these people come to him, he has a singing delight over them and wants to open out all the best to them." Like the Prodigal Son, Graham added in his own mind. The Father's love was targeted on the returning son. The world, his friends, had taken everything from him, and thrown him aside, but the Father gave the best ...

The best. The ring, the best robes, the fatted calf ... the

best. Graham could picture all these things, but by that time he had had enough of passing on his mother's love message to Sheleen. He wanted to be the one to give her comfort; not his mother, and not God.

He tried to reach out to her again but she drew nervously away from him, as though he were a visitor from another planet. Why couldn't he be smooth and macho, he despaired, spewing out self-confidence and charm? A bit of soap-opera magic was sadly lacking here.

But finally, the calm she had been building up so carefully, shattered.

"I couldn't believe it at first," she whispered. "I thought she - Granny - was only being spiteful. And then I looked at the big family photograph on the bureau and I knew. I knew. I wasn't one of them. It was suddenly so obvious. How couldn't I have seen it before?"

Then her breath came in ragged gasps, and the tears came with the suddenness of a dam bursting. Graham held her through the storm, willing the hurt in her to stop.

"I'm glad I could be here with you," he said at last, but the words didn't have the desired effect.

Sheleen got up and sat facing opposite him and there was a special gentleness in her voice when she finally spoke. "I'm not good at expressing myself, Graham, and I don't want to hurt your feelings. But tonight, right now, I need to be alone. If I had to choose someone to comfort me, it would be you, believe me! But it's not - how can I put this? - it's not just human comfort I need. I need to get right with God."

There was something courageous and raw and fearless that stood out in that lovely face and Graham struggled to understand her words.

"You see, it's not just learning that I'm adopted. As much as I can, I accept that, and in their own way I know my parents love me just as much as they love my brothers. But ... I suppose that I've been frightened. "

"You've been frightened?" Graham felt as if he had missed part of the conversation. "What have you been frightened of, Sheleen?"

"It's hard to say. For ages now I've been frightened of not finding my way, of not finding ... oh, I don't know ... something that gives meaning to my life. I pinned all my hopes on people; my parents, my brothers - especially Timothy - and you, Graham. And it's as if, one by one, all these props have been knocked aside."

"But it was only a misunderstanding that set us apart, Sheleen," Graham protested, dismissing the weeks of silence with a flick of his hand.

She looked strangely blank, and he knew he hadn't connected up with her train of thought. Instead, she went on, "Perhaps it's as if my hands have been too full and God had to show me what it was like to be empty and confused, and then he could step in ... something like that."

"You mean, it's as if God was saying, 'Right, first I have

to get her attention'," Graham said, watching the silent interplay of emotions on her face.

"Yes."

Graham added more peats to the fire and stared down into the glowing world of brilliant orange and yellow.

He bent towards the warmth as if towards succour. Without turning around, he said, "You're not the only one on the injured list, Sheleen. My mother overheard a conversation between you and your mother, and in it I figured as a pleasant way of spending summer. Never anything more than that."

"Oh, Graham, I'd no idea!"

"Look, sorry... forget I said that. I didn't mean to match your problems with mine."

"I only agreed with Mum because" - A pause, then she looked up suddenly - "because if I let her know how I *really* felt about you, she'd be anxious. We were too young, too far apart socially, geographically, and so on. But after everything that's happened recently, she's changed her mind."

"There's no problem, then - for us, I mean?" He moved nearer to her, but she held out her hand in a gesture which was unmistakable in any language - 'No further'.

"Would you do something for me, Graham?"

"Yes, anything."

"You say yes without even knowing what I'm going to

90

ask," she said, with a half-smile.

"I draw the line at walking back through that mist again! Anyway, no-one will expect us back till the mist lifts. Uh, what do you want?"

"Leave me alone just now. Go to James's shieling. You can light a fire there, can't you? Please?" She demanded it of him, fiercely, and Graham stood up awkwardly, wanting to say something more, but not quite knowing what.

He waited for her to continue, thinking, "How could a girl be so sure? So - adamant?"

And, as if reading what was in his eyes and on his face, Sheleen went on, "I knew this would happen when you appeared tonight; I knew you'd distract me. We'll talk another time. Tonight I must think about my life; like your mother said, 'Who I am and whose I am'."

"So, tossed in the 'Unwanted Basket' with one grand statement. How could anyone compete with *that*?" Graham thought bitterly, and let the sick disappointment sweep over him.

Leaving Sheleen, he crossed over to James' shieling and went in. He felt like getting mad and slamming around the building for a while. Instead, not bothering to light a fire, he lay down on the hard earth and closed his eyes, not willing to face whatever thoughts might come in the darkness.

CHAPTER 11

DRENCHED IN JOY

Graham awoke once in the dank pre-dawn gloom and felt the damp of the earth below him passing through the fabric of his clothes. His left leg was crippled with cramp and one arm seemed to have stayed asleep. Shivering, he listened to the lonely cry of a curlew. The silence of the moorland was so solid you could almost lean against it.

He tried to imagine the time when the small settlement of shielings had been full of life. Now, the same moorland no longer heard the laughter of children, or the lively discussions between the adults, or the lowing of cows as they came home for the evening milking. Now there was only an eerie silence leaving Graham alone with his thoughts which were, at that moment, mostly about how unfair everything was.

A long time passed before he eventually got up and opened the shieling door. Night had travelled on, and now the first glow of light had fanned up behind the eastern hills and filtered into the sky. The birds were singing harmoniously, keeping in tune with the rhythm of the river.

Picking up his haversack, he went next door and woke up the sleeping Sheleen. After sharing a Mars Bar and can of Coke, they both emerged stiffly into the cold morning light. Dew lay thick on the heather and the air had that early, fresh, unused feeling.

"A brand new day," Sheleen said, flicking her hair out of her eyes.

"Aha, my pin-up girl has lost some of her gloss over-night!" Graham said teasingly. "You've got the unwashed and unironed look; your hair looks as if you've been pulled through a hedge backwards, and you've got dirt on your forehead."

He reached out with his fingertip as though to rub it off. And then, as she stood there looking up at him, the teasing look faded from his eyes and he put his hands in his pocket.

He looked down at some tiny yellow flowers which opened in buttery clots against bare black soil. Without looking up, he said, "Did you ... work everything out?"

"No, I didn't. It was all worked out for me. Okay, so maybe I don't know right now who my real parents are. Maybe, one day, I'll want to find out - who knows? But this morning, and from now on, I can call Jesus 'My Lord and my God'. That's so personal, so one-to-one, that I wouldn't waste time drumming up an identity crisis now!"

He did not reply, but closed up the shieling door and slung the haversack onto his back. They began to walk towards an eastern arc of sky still submerged in the afterglow of sunrise and Graham was filled with a sense of how mysterious and beautiful the world was.

Something in what Sheleen had just said stirred in him more of that feeling of beauty and mystery; he recognized it without fully knowing what he felt.

"Testing ... Testing ... Anybody there?" Sheleen asked, looking at him. Her clear, frank gaze was unnerving.

What could he say? - 'I feel as if something, some stir of promise in our relationship, has been knocked again out of my reach. Now I'm drifting, unsteady, uncertain. I don't know what the score is.' No, he couldn't say that.

Instead, he said, "Well, you look as if you're happy now. So, maybe I'm a little bit jealous. Here I am, a big ball of guilt inside me ... "

"Guilt?"

Sheleen looked into those grey eyes which normally were so full of light and laughter and now ached with a kind of shame.

He told her about the poaching sessions, how he had apologized to her father, but couldn't bring himself to tell his own mother.

"You see, it's not really the poaching I feel so terrible about - I can sort of justify that, well, almost! But using my mother as an informer! I've got to tell her and I can picture the look on her face when I do and I don't think I can bear it."

Sheleen reached out with her hand and lifted his chin slightly, forcing him to look at her straight in the eye. When he did, it was to see the ache inside him reflected in her face, and he realized that she was willing to share even that with him.

"I can be there with you when you tell her," she said. "And Graham, what about James? Shouldn't you tackle him after you've told your mother? If he realizes that your mother and my father both know the truth then ... that emotional blackmail stuff can be dumped in the 'Out' tray."

"Suppose so." He hesitated before he went on, "You know, it hurts when you see a chink in your mentor's armour, doesn't it? But it's not so bad when the whole armour falls off and he shows himself to be ... uh, how can I describe him?"

"Try 'Crazy'?"

"Oh, c'mon, it's not like you to be a master of overstatement! And anyway, Sheleen, where's your new-found Christian charity? He's not that bad!"

"That bad? Tell me about it! You know why my father sacked him from his summer job at the Estate? He tried to stir up a mini-revolution amongst the staff. Fed them with a few strains of Marxism. Said they were earning half the wages our English staff get, and other lies like the Lodge being renovated with Local Authority money. We had to show a few of the staff some written facts before they all did a mass exit."

"Oh-ho, so that's why he's so bitter," Graham thought as Sheleen continued.

"We found out afterwards that James was a bit light-fingered. Apparently that's why he was thrown out of Uni. But, to be fair, he must have outgrown that hobby when he was working for us!"

"And he made up for it this summer," Graham said grimly. Mentally, he put James away and shut the drawer on him. They walked on through the wild, lonely and lovely land. Dawn had now given way to full-fledged morning. Against a huge silence of moorland, the tiniest sounds were as startling as gun-shot. The haunting cry of a bird. The splash of a fish. The sound of Sheleen's voice when she picked up on the conversation.

"James used to give me a real jaundiced feeling, but now, I only feel pity for him. Sure, material security can add a lot to a person's peace of mind - up to a point. Past that, it's a false hope, and I know what I'm talking about!"

"Mmmm. My philosophy is to plug up all possible cracks in my life where poverty could creep in. Education is one way - get a good job, and so on. My mother agrees, then spoils it by trotting out wise and wonderful phrases like 'Money is a passport for everything but happiness, and a passport everywhere but to heaven.' "

"You could sound a bit more convinced, couldn't you?"

"I'm not very convinced of anything right now, Sheleen. I only know that we - the two of us - are separated again, but this time it's not by money or misunderstanding or anything as simple as that."

As they navigated round some boggy areas, he waited for her to reply, but she didn't have any answer for him, so he went on. "Last summer, we were just cruising along. Everything was fine, wasn't it? - now it's all so complicated." He struggled to make his voice sound light and playful. "Go on, say 'I guess that's life, kiddo'. "

She did not reply, but stopped to gaze down into the still water of the river. It looked as if bits of the sky had fallen into the water and were now melting. Graham saw their own reflections, wavering a little, side by side and close together. "The closeness is all an illusion," he thought, "because I've never felt so apart from her as I do now. She's got peace of mind. She seems drenched in joy. As for me ...?"

He lobbed a stone into the water aggressively and their reflection became distorted, and then shattered completely.

CHAPTER TWELVE

SO TELL ME!

Over the next few days Graham felt that the ripples on the surface of his life had smoothed out. Timothy's recovery was as startling as only a child's can be, and he was expected to be released from hospital any day now. Graham had also done his confessional bit with his mother, and Sheleen had been a support to him, just as she had promised. His mother had forgiven his poaching escapade, but that was a couple of nights ago, and this evening she was in a less-than-forgiving mood.

"Your room, Graham. It's a tip."

"First prize for understatement of the year, Mum," he replied absently. He was sprawled on the couch watching an ancient black-and-white Western on TV. "This is boring! It's got about the same excitement level as watching corn grow. It's - "

"Don't change the subject! You've only got two more days at home - and when are you going to sort out your clothes. They're everywhere but in the drawers!"

"Typical female over-reaction, Mum - I mean, excuse me for actually sleeping up there! Anyway, what's exactly wrong with the lived-in look?"

He ducked as his mother threw a cushion at him. "And don't worry about the gear I'm taking away to college. It's all in there somewhere, isn't it?"

"Finding it is the only problem! Oh Graham ... " Mrs Maclean said with an exaggerated air of patience. "How will you manage without me?"

"Easy, Mum, easy!" he laughed, throwing the cushion up in the air. "You're the one who's going to have the withdrawal symptoms. What will you get all hyped-up about then? I'm sure Samuel will keep his ... uh, your room all neat as a new pin!"

"I'll only find that out in time, my son," she smiled at his rudeness. "Oh, why am I wasting my breath talking to you? Nagging is bad for my self-esteem and it gets me nowhere fast."

Graham unfolded his long legs and crossed over to her. "Ah-hem, Mrs Maclean," he counselled her in his most soothing imitation of a psychiatrist. "By your aggression I think you may be covering up a more deep-seated problem. Your nagging is a safety valve. It takes your mind off the empty house you'll have in a couple of days, the closed chapter in your life. " Adding, in his own voice, "And stops you being marshmallowy and soft, right?"

She laughed outright at his attempt to rubbish her fears.

"You've got a sort of infectious daftness, you know that? And, since when did you call up this new psychiatric ability?"

"Since I realised that all the time you're nag-nag-nag you're trying desperately to stay buttoned up and British."

"Graham, there's something I want to say to you," his mother said, cutting the psychoanalysis short. She began to fiddle with her wedding ring so she could talk without looking up. Graham, aware that it's sometimes easier not to look at someone when you're talking, knew it was something important.

"Oh-oh. Why do I get the feeling you're wanting a serious talk, Mum?" he questioned her, teasingly.

"Because you know me well enough by now?" she retorted, but her laughter faded in her eyes. "Just one statement, that's all! It'll save me saying it, you know, later. When your father died, Graham, I wanted to die with him. I felt my life was over ... finished. Those awful first few weeks I used to stand at the gate in the evenings, looking out at these wide open fields and empty moorland. And I would know, that nowhere, in all that space would I ever see my husband. Not hear his voice, not see his walk, not anything. Nothing. I'd sort of chant to myself, 'He's dead. He's dead.' Why can't you believe he's dead?' "

Graham shot his mother an uneasy look, but she either didn't catch it, or she chose to ignore it. She went on, "But there was you ... and you needed me and you gave me the reason to go on at that time. Later, when I became a Christian, I found that, in Christ, there was everything to live for. There was a deeper reason to go on. But ..." she hesitated, her head cocked in a way that was habitual with her, as if she was never quite sure she was being understood. "But, what I'm trying to say is ... if it wasn't for you, Graham ... those first few years ... "

"Wait a minute, " Graham said breezily, as he tried to bring humour into a situation which, he felt, was in danger of going into emotional overload. "You said *one* statement."

"But it had many parts!" She tweaked his cheek playfully. "I knew it. I just knew it! Saying I love you, I'll miss you, I'll think of you all the time - you can't cope with corny numbers like that, can you? Am I right?"

"Oh, Mum!" Graham felt the pressure on him to say something cool and unsentimental, but all he could manage was, "I'm looking for something wise to say, but nothing comes to mind. But - but because I don't trot out the right words, it doesn't mean a thing. I just find it ... hard. You know that, don't you?"

For a moment there was a profound silence as they both contemplated that past and that future.

Graham broke the silence. "However, however and however, all this isn't going to clear my bedroom, is it? Right! Operation Bomb-site is about to be launched ... but first, make us a sandwich."

"Oh, you!" she lamented, but obediently scurried into the kitchen. From there came the muffled sounds of clattering cups, the swing of the fridge door, the kettle hissing.

Then, above that, he heard the outside door open and a familiar voice calling, "Anyone in?" It was Sheleen.

Expecting her to come into the living room immediately, he leaned against the window ledge, jamming his hands down into the pockets of his jeans and stretching his legs out in front of him. Sheleen, however, stayed in the kitchen with his mother, and the burr of their conversation drifted towards him. After a while, Graham tired of the nonchalant position and shuffled closer to the door.

"...so, you see, Sheleen," his mother was saying, "your birth, your life, was never a mistake in God's eyes. He was the one who formed you in your mother's womb; he knew you before you were ever born. Isn't that a tremendous thought?"

Sheleen's voice was too soft and low for him to catch the reply, but he eventually heard that familiar ripple of laughter in her voice and decided that it was safe to join them. When he saw her, he noticed again that look of calm amazement, the look that had first appeared in her face on their walk back from the shielings. Then, like now, she appeared to have just awakened from a beautiful dream.

"Hi, Graham!" The smile was in her voice and in her wide eyes also, but she continued leaning conspiratorially towards his mother across the kitchen table. Between them there was a subtle interplay of sharing and agreement, of a fellowship which transcended age and class differences. Feeling a complete outsider, Graham made a vague grunty noise which could have been a 'hello'.

He thought he might allow himself a little comment on the new closeness between Sheleen and his mother. Listening to their continuing conversation, he spooned coffee into three mugs and said casually, "What d'you think of this philosophy, Sheleen - 'a teenager shouldn't be in agreement with anyone over thirty-five?' Could be thought very uncool to socialise with your friend's parents!"

As he sat down and handed them the stoneware coffee mugs, Mrs Maclean flicked a glance towards her son's face. She was trying not to smile. Sheleen started laughing instead of saying anything, and a hot flame of jealousy shot through Graham. What's so funny? he demanded silently.

"That philosophy - as you call it - sounds strongly of James," his mother said. Her voice was patient and slow as if she were talking to a nervous child. "For James, it's essential to rebel against something, anything. He gives everybody the impression he doesn't care for them, or their little values - that way, he can feel superior to them. I'm sure it's a psychological device to cope with his own hang-ups, and inadequacies."

"Wow! that's a world-shattering analysis if ever I heard one!" Graham gulped down some coffee and chomped into a cheese sandwich, then went on, "Okay, I admit he's not exactly the true gentleman, but ... when I was fishing with him and playing football and just hanging about with the rest of the guys, well, I felt I belonged somewhere."

"Even when he was doing wrong?" Mrs Maclean prompted, but not hurriedly, as if they had all evening to discuss it.

An uncomfortable thought began skittering around in his mind. If it would just hold still for one second, he might be able to capture it. Chewing and swallowing each unhungry mouthful, his mind drifting to that last night with James, he suddenly wanted not to care where exactly he belonged.

"Graham?" Sheleen said in a soft, funny voice.

He turned his head to face her, his eyes burning. This was a new experience. Totally new. New to have Sheleen and his mother sharing something he couldn't enter into; and it wasn't a comfortable feeling by any stretch of the imagination. Putting down his mug so fast that the liquid slopped over onto the table, he scraped back his chair and said, "Okay, so I wasn't over-thrilled by James' antics ... so it was really all about seconds of excitement scattered in months of boredom ... so I had to grovel on the carpet and apologise to the world and his wife. So, tell me then, where do I belong? I definitely don't belong in your little Christian world, do I? See, I can sense you both adjusting your talk as if I was someone to ... some kid who doesn't know too much."

He paused, finished emphatically and very slowly, as if to give added meaning to his words, "So, tell me where I belong, because I'll be blowed if I know!"

CHAPTER 13

THE DISTORTED REFLECTION

Riding the waves of his own anger, Graham bolted out of the house. He strode over to the barn and leaned against its rough, stone wall, needing the silence and the feel of the weeping, damp evening. He sniffed the earth-smells of autumn, and listened to a nearby sheep snacking off the lush grass. Above, a flock of birds made their evening journey home, twittering to one another.

"You wally! You complete wally!" he reproached himself!" Each 'wally' was underscored by a clenched fist slamming at the barn door. Finally, he drew a long breath and willed himself to relax. Rehashing problems wouldn't solve anything, he thought as he looked at the distant hills, watching the light move on them, changing from grey to misty blue to purple.

The air was cool and nipped at his face. It was getting colder now, the year was moving on. Soon he would be at college in Edinburgh; and Sheleen? Where would she end up? Probably anywhere that put a good thousand

2 FREE BOOKS
AND A SURPRISE GIFT

We would like to take this opportunity to thank you for reading this Mills & Boon® book by offering you the chance to take TWO more specially selected books from the Medical™ series absolutely FREE! We're also making this offer to introduce you to the benefits of the Mills & Boon® Book Club™—

- **FREE home delivery**
- **FREE gifts and competitions**
- **FREE monthly Newsletter**
- **Exclusive Mills & Boon Book Club offers**
- **Books available before they're in the shops**

Accepting these FREE books and gift places you under no obligation to buy, you may cancel at any time, even after receiving your free books. Simply complete your details below and return the entire page to the address below. You don't even need a stamp!

YES Please send me 2 free Medical books and a surprise gift. I understand that unless you hear from me, I will receive 5 superb new stories every month including two 2-in-1 books priced at £5.30 each and a single book priced at £3.30, postage and packing free. I am under no obligation to purchase any books and may cancel my subscription at any time. The free books and gift will be mine to keep in any case.

Ms/Mrs/Miss/Mr _____ Initials _____

_____

Surname _____

Address _____

_____

_____ Postcode _____

E-mail _____

Send this whole page to: Mills & Boon Book Club, Free Book Offer, FREEPOST NAT 10298, Richmond, TW9 1BR miles between herself and his own emotional performances, he thought bitterly.

And then as if by thinking about her, he had somehow called her up. And she was there, coming towards him.

"Okay?" Sheleen asked, as she came up beside him. Her voice was hesitant and unsure.

Graham nodded. "Don't get mad at me. I'm mad enough for both of us, so don't try and take the credit!"

A little smile lifted the corners of her mouth. "No, I'm sorry for, you know, making you feel out of it. Forgive me?"

Allowing the relief to creep over his face, he retorted, "What do you think?" Then he moved slightly so that they were close together, voices low, heads almost meeting. He said, "Sorry for using you both as a yelling board. I suppose I'm not the regular bucket of fun I used to be - so, my plea is temporary insanity!"

"Neither of us are. What we used to be - that is."

Aware again of the body blow dealt by the adoption revelation, his hands touched her's by instinct. His thoughts were in knots. What does a guy do when he's trying to tell a girl a million things which really mean he needs her? And he wants to be needed by her? Just because I'm not up to making sentimental pleas, he thought grimly, doesn't mean the feelings aren't there inside me.

Aloud, he said, "Sheleen, want to walk for a bit? We could talk or, if you prefer, silence?" And he mimed a zipping motion of his mouth.

She answered with a nod and the birth of another smile. "Sure! But not too far. Samuel Stern is coming to your house tonight, your mum says. I'm dying to see him, you know, to tell him about, well, finding Jesus. Or is it being found by Jesus?"

Walking over the faint dampness that veiled the ground, they reached the wide free spaces outside Mrs Maclean's garden, and Sheleen continued, almost apologetically, "So you won't mind if I backtrack when Samuel comes, will you? You know what it's like!"

"No, actually, I don't know what it's like." Graham gave her a very level glance, and her eyes wavered and dropped suddenly.

Her eyes stayed down but she said, "Graham. Graham, if I could just tell you what it's like to have a personal relationship with God ... if I could just grab you and take you to him - "

"But you can't, and that's that," he said flatly. He couldn't stand to hear her stumble around in that way. He couldn't stand to hear her say the words.

"Okay, I get the message! Hold off, will you?" Sheleen, backing away, put up her hands in mock surrender. "Sorry I touched your antennae, sir! Subject number one discussed and disposed of. Second item on the agenda?" and she ticked off two fingers.

Graham began to laugh, inside and out. At the same time, Sheleen tripped backwards over a stone and he had

108

to move quickly to rescue her from becoming a crumpled heap on the grass.

"That's one extravagant gesture, Sheleen," he teased. "You don't really have to fall at my feet, you know. But if you insist."

"Ha, ha. You should be so lucky!" she retorted, her eyes singing out a smile. Graham had all of thirty seconds to enjoy the moment and then they were off again, walking towards the nearby loch. Its banks were thickly fringed with fading yellow flag irises and marshmarigolds; but looking at them in the distance, in the closing dusk, the flowers were a white blur.

"Last night, I had a dream," Sheleen eventually spoke into the silence. Her voice was almost whispery, and it was as if she were not talking to anyone but to herself. "I dreamt that I was in a huge shopping centre; all steel and mirrored glass and fountains and escalators, you know the kind I mean?" Graham shook his head, waiting for her to go on, knowing it was important.

"No, of course you don't, Graham," she continued, "but by next week you'll be an old hand at riding the escalators in Edinburgh. Anyway, my dream. I dreamt of following a woman's figure up all the escalators, all the way up to the top of the building. I was sure it was someone I knew very well. Every time I was in position to see her face clearly in all the mirrors, the reflection became sort of ... distorted. I woke up feeling that I called out a name ... but I couldn't remember what name." Sheleen's voice trailed off, as if embarrassed at her own words.

"Could it have been your, um, biological mother you were following?" Graham paused, picking his words with delicate care. "Your real mother, I mean. No, that's not right either! Leanda Pugh-Smith is as real to you as any mother could be, isn't she? Your birth mother, then. Could it have been her?"

Sheleen gave a hesitant nod. "I guess so. Then, when I woke up, I wondered what I really would say if I met her."

Graham screwed up his eyes, thinking hard, thinking in mental capital letters of 'What if She Hadn't Been Born.' His grey eyes turned on her broodingly.

"How about, 'Thank you for not aborting me. Thank you for all the hard times you must have gone through to allow me to live. Thank you for the chance of life. Thank you - ' "

Those luminous eyes filmed with tears as she interrupted him. "Oh Graham! What a beautiful thing to say. I never thought of it like that. I was going to say to her ..." She stopped in her tracks and stood still, her eyes looking far off into the water of the loch. "I was going to say to my ... uh, the birth mother, "Okay, so maybe your life was in knots and I - the baby 'I' - had obviously chosen an inconvenient moment to make my debut, but, what was so bad that you could give up your own flesh and blood? Your baby?' And I would ask her, 'Did you look at me - the baby

110

me - before disposing of that unwanted member? Did you ever hold me, cuddle me, touch me?' "

Graham's heart went out to her, not only with love but with an almost brotherly compassion.

"Don't worry, Graham," she said, as if in answer to his thoughts. "I'm not falling apart at the seams over this, honestly."

She tried to re-arrange her face into a brighter expression before asking, "It's not too serious a crime to want to ask a couple of questions, is it? Like, why was I given up for adoption? Was it because I interrupted education, or a promising career, or what? Or was it because I was a result of too much alcohol at some wild party and I didn't ... didn't mean anything?"

"Oh, Sheleen ... " Graham began, only to be chopped off as she made a fretful movement.

"Please, please understand, Graham. Nothing can ever take away the knowledge that God is saying to me in the Bible, things like 'I love you. You are very special to me. You are mine.' Nothing can take that away. But, family-wise, I've lost a feeling of connectedness - if there is such a word."

"Look, Sheleen, I think I understand," Graham said, turning her to face him squarely. The closeness of the moment gave him confidence. "It's like, well, you want a link, a handshake type of thing from another generation."

"A link?"

"Yes. Take what my mother said today, for example. I was combing back my hair with my fingers, like this ," and he demonstrated the act, "and Mum said, 'Oh, you're so like your father when you do that, he did that all the time.' And it made me feel good that my mum saw my father in my actions."

"You've got it! That's exactly what I mean." Sheleen cried. "And when Mum and Dad and Timothy come home tomorrow and we'll all be seated around the dining room table, everything will be the same, and yet everything has completely, totally changed. I'll see Timothy as like Mum, but with my father's mannerisms; and I'll look across at the mirror and wonder where I got my green eyes from, and - " she tugged harshly at her fringe "and this colour hair."

Turning slightly, so that she was leaning her head against his shoulder, she ventured, "Graham, is it silly to wonder if there's someone out there with eyes and features a variation of my own? To wonder about it, and keep on wondering, even during the night? Tell me honestly - is that silly?"

Silence reigned, deep and reluctant, while Graham tried desperately to find something to say. He felt he was being led to a place in her mind where he had no guidelines, no map of directions.

As they stood there, the sound of a car reached faintly across the loch, headlights flashed across the water like the searchlights in a television thriller, then the sound grew louder as the car passed them.

"That's Samuel," Sheleen said, disengaging herself. "Let's go back."

"You go, Sheleen. I want to go for a run."

"A run? You mean - a run? As in, going nowhere in particular?" she asked, and Graham searched for the teasing note in her voice, but it wasn't there.

She was genuinely puzzled. "Hey, Graham, I thought you islanders had enough outdoor activity without having to manufacture more!"

"Shows how much you Sassenachs know about us!" he grinned, explaining, "I want enough fresh air to last me through to next year."

What he meant was, "I need to get away from you and Mum and Samuel for a while. I feel I'm outside some circle, while you're all on the inside."

Parting with a "see you later", Graham broke into a run, more of a gallop than a jog. He streaked along, with no particular destination in mind, aware of the presence of things surrounding him, small scatterings of disturbed animals and birds, sensations of frightened movement.

Graham didn't know, then, of nearby furtive movement on a human level. That still awaited him.

CHAPTER 14

RUN HOME THEN!

When he had run himself out, Graham stopped. Breathing through his mouth, his chest heaving, at first he could hardly focus his eyes on anything. Aware that he was now at the far end of the loch and quite near the Lodge, he allowed some self mockery. 'So much for Sheleen saying that I was running nowhere in particular. My legs must be on automatic pilot!'

His thoughts were broken by the sight of a figure, emerging from amongst the clump of trees leading to the Lodge. It was James.

"James! Hang on a minute!" Graham shouted.

James looked around casually, and then not so casually. He looked round as if he were searching for a means of escape.

'That bad to see me, huh?' Graham thought, and the realisation that their friendship was now stone-cold dead made him feel bad, as if he tasted something bitter.

"Well, well!" James drawled, as Graham approached

him. "Risking soiling your lily-white reputation by talking to me? Big of you!"

"Oh, you're an expert on my reputation now?" Graham responded to that flat cold-tinged voice. "Sounds as if I've been crossed off your Christmas card list."

"Got it in one! You know something, Graham-boy, you're a million miles less fun than when you took up with those toffs. All posh and la-di-da. And you weren't that much fun to begin with!"

Graham had the passing thought that it would be nice to rub James' nose in the peat-soil.

"Is that Sheleen you're talking about?" he asked, drilling James with a hateful look.

"She's one of them." James lit a cigarette and dragged savagely on it, blowing out a voluptuous stream of smoke. "Okay, so she's nicely thrown together, but all that good breeding and gentility - yeuch, makes me want to throw up!"

He suddenly laughed, although it didn't sound like a laugh, belonging more to the snarl family. "And now - what d'you know - hasn't sweet Sheleen turned out to be yet another emotional cripple with religion as a crutch. So you're definitely barking up the wrong girl, aren't you?"

Graham felt the pressure on him to crack James across the face open-handed, but resisted. Instead he gave him a shove, saying, "Go and bore someone else, will you? Anyway, if you hate them all that much - " another shove, "what's your face doing around here?"

"My face goes where I go!" James hissed, and sprang forward.

Graham, sidestepping neatly, left James to plunge downwards, grabbing at air. He fell to the ground, swearing, snarling, and then began to pick himself up, rising to one knee.

"D'you want to end up spitting teeth, you traitor?"

The voice, now like the snapping of a whip, assaulted Graham's ears. He could feel James' breath on his face. He didn't reply, and everything was still around them as if all the little animals and birds were holding their breath.

"C'mon," James taunted, "c'mon, I'm dying to see your face come unglued. C'mon!"

"Look, save the soft talk for later," Graham said, taking a few backwards steps. "Your power to charm scares me, y'know that? And all I really wanted was to put a few things straight with you. That's all." Stopping decisively where he was, he added, "So there's no need to invade my private space, is there?"

"Oh, I say, how super!" James replied in his best English accent, but he stopped momentarily for a drag at his rescued cigarette, and blew out a vague spiral into the cool air. "Aw, why do I bother? You're a lost cause. You know, you're even beginning to *sound* like the Puke-Smiths. Your knees must be sore with all that crawling."

"And your tongue must be warped with all that lying."

"What lies?" James' face seemed cut from stone, and the eyes he turned on Graham were hard and suspicious, his voice like a grey steel knife.

"As if you didn't know!" The storm of Graham's voice seemed to fill even the great outdoors as he went on, "You bamboozled me with all those lies, patched up with bits of truth. The Estate wages, the Improvement Grants ... and a heap of other things. Everything except the whole truth. You wouldn't know the truth if it jumped up and bit you on the nose!"

James drew back from Graham's anger, as if he could get further away from the onslaught of words hurtled at him. Then he retaliated with a string of sheer blasphemy, his voice rising to drown out that of his former friend.

Deep inside him, at the very edge of consciousness, Graham felt a sudden flicker of emotion. It was pain. And with it, the memory of Samuel Stern's words, 'Somebody swore using his name, and it hurt me so much, it was like a physical pain. Can you understand that, Graham?' He couldn't, then, but now, in an instant, he could understand.

He knew that subtly he had passed over some invisible line. Not yet committed to that Name, but no longer indifferent. The relationship between him and that Name would and must alter.

The tirade of scorn was still going on in his ear. Graham pressed his lips together and then moved forward. letting his breath out in a soft hiss.

"Any more compliments? This has got to be good for my ego - only I don't worry about the opinions of people I can't respect. Especially a fugitive from a puzzle factory like you."

James made a sudden movement, quickly suppressed. He gazed at Graham for a moment, his jaw tightening with anger. He jerked an obscene gesture and Graham responded with one of the phrases they had both said to others in the past.

It was not a plunge into nostalgia, but now the final irony in their relationship. "Adios, amigo. Nice knowing you. Pleasure forgetting you."

"Scram. Vamoose!" James spat out, before wheeling round and walking back towards the trees. And then, over his shoulder, "Run home then, prodigal son,"

For a sharp moment, all Graham could do was to stare at the youth's retreating back. How little James could have guessed the effect his flippant words had on him. The words loomed out - 'Run home then, prodigal son' - and stalked huge and meaningful through the muddle of his thoughts.

A space seemed to open in his mind; light poured in, a clear white light, and for a moment he stood in the centre of that light. The protective wall of denial began to tumble down, and as the bricks crumbled, there was nothing left but reality.

Like the prodigal son of old, 'he came to himself' and received all that was kept aside for the returning son. The forgiveness. The rightful place in the family of God. It poured out from the Father, lavishly, extravagantly, without stopping.

As he looked up into the night sky, Graham whispered, "No more running. I've come home."

CHAPTER 15

THE BATTLE OF THE BARN

For a long time Graham stood there, wanting to gather the moment to himself, to curl his thoughts permanently round this memory, this night. His heart was filled to bursting with - what? What label could be pinned on it? He couldn't put a name to it. All he knew was that, inside him, he wanted to laugh, to cry, to write a song, to leap with joy.

Instead he remained motionless, drinking in the peacefulness of his surroundings. It matched his mood. A thin moon injected its luminous glow into the slowly darkening sky. Its lights struck a gleam on the surface of the loch. Yet beyond the clump of trees there was a wide, unmoving darkness. Except for one faint movement.

It was a little thing, lasting only a fraction of a second, but it made Graham break off his train of thought. James was still there in the trees. But why? Was he, for some reason, waiting for him to go? That would explain why he had backtracked, instead of going in the original direction.

Graham stood cemented in place, as his mind suddenly began to shift gears. James was surely up to something. 'I'll move away, watch, and then follow him,' he finally decided. As he made his way up towards a large boulder which would give him a bit of cover, he could feel the blood pounding in his veins. His fists clenched into tiny knots, but after crouching behind the boulder for a long moment, he began to relax. After all, he wasn't alone now.

Then, abruptly, everything was jerked into frantic motion. A surge of movement in the darkness of the trees caught Graham's eye. As he squinted in that direction James emerged from his hiding place and ran silently and swiftly towards the Estate barn. By the time he slid open the massive doors Graham had found his legs taking over from his brain. Without having made a conscious decision to do so, he started to run through the shadowy light.

Diving for the protection of the trees, he zig-zagged, keeping to the shadows, staying low. James could reappear at any moment, and Graham wanted to remain unseen, just like the Western heroes he had seen in a hundred films.

Once at the barn he hesitated, not quite sure what to do next. Then he crept through the open door. He stood still for a minute, letting his eyes grow accustomed to the dimness. Pushing some cobwebs away, he waited until he found his twilight vision. Here was darkness and silence, and the still smell of unused, dusty air. Animals were no longer kept there, Graham knew, but the hay for feeding the horses was at one end.

The silence was broken by the sound of pouring liquid and then, as the place was suddenly lit up by the flare of a cigarette lighter, the air was permeated with the smell of petrol. The shadows began to lift from Graham's head as he felt rage rising up from the pit of his stomach, coursing through him like a floodtide.

There seemed to be a million miles of floor space between them. Without being aware that he had moved, Graham found himself standing directly opposite James. The shock of his former friend's actions had propelled him across the room as if he had been catapulted.

James, who had been targeting the cigarette lighter down towards the hay, wheeled round. But it was too late, for Graham had got him around the knees in a low tackle. Although he did not manage to send James flying into the hay bales, he did knock him off balance.

"For Pete's sake, what are you up to?" Graham shouted, as he kicked the lighter out of James' hand and sent it rattling across the stone floor. He could hardly see now in the frail light. The sliver of moonlight through the open door made little difference.

And yet he did see the coming movement and his body tensed. The fist exploded in his face and he staggered backwards, sprawling across the floor. Picking himself up, he clambered on top of a hay bale, and jumping, leapt onto James' retreating back. But the older youth spun him round almost effortlessly, and with one cruel movement, sent Graham flying through the air, striking the hay bales with a sickening thud. Then he was pulled up again and James slugged him square in the middle with all his strength.

"One word about this and even your problems will have problems, *mate*," James hissed. "Sheleen, your mother - y'know what I mean? *They'll* have problems." He dried the sweat on his face with the back of his sleeve, appearing totally wiped out after the whole tough-guy routine. He looked about him, a kind of desperation in his movements.

"No, on second thoughts ... " Twisting round, he scooped up the petrol-drenched hay, the lighter and the container. "This never even happened. It was all a figment of your imagination. Get it?"

With that, he disappeared into the night, briefly becoming a grotesque moonlit silhouette in the barn door.

Graham became aware of a moan, like the noise made by a wounded animal, and knew that it came from himself. Doubled up, he sat on the hard stone floor, wheezing; waiting for his heart to resume its normal beating, trying to collect his scattered senses and to work out which part of his body protested the most.

For a strange moment he felt as if he were a mere spectator in a drama, taking no more than a half-hearted interest in his own fate. Slowly, cautiously, he dragged the mass of aching muscle into a half-standing position. The anger which had seconds before run through his blood, now evaporated. A shudder went through him, not of fear, but of gratitude.

'Okay, so fighting isn't the best way to start off my Christian life,' he thought, 'even though James must be right out of his brain to pull a stunt like that. But - God *used* me there. Unbelievable!'

The relief that swept over him seemed to drain all the strength from his body. He was gasping like a half-drowned swimmer and, taking that first step, his legs felt rubbery and loose-jointed.

His legs did manage to carry him home, however. Home to Sheleen and his mother and Samuel. Home to advice, home to sharing. Eventually, he saw the distant oblongs of light stream from the house across the dark ground.

"Only another hundred yards," he groaned aloud. Every step seemed to bring a fresh wave of pain, and his jaw still tingled from the fight. "Only ...! Go on, Graham old man, you can ... "

"Graham? Graham!" Sheleen came running to meet him, down the path and out into the road. A slight breeze blew her denim jacket behind her and ruffled her hair. "What took you so long? Where did you run to? I've got

..." She broke off and looked at him, amazed. "Wow! You look whacked. If that's what running does to you, I suggest you take up knitting!"

He rested his hand on her shoulder, as if her body was a walking stick to support him. Grinning, he said, "Have I got news for you."

"Graham, wait till you hear this."

"Go on then, ladies first."

"Huh - since when? No ... what's your news? I mean, you look the way I ended my stories when I was in primary. Everyone was always 'tired but happy'. So, c'mon, don't keep me in suspense."

They both laughed, and the warmth of shared laughter enveloped them until Graham said, "No, honestly! It's something I want to tell you, my mother and Samuel. So, over to you, Sheleen."

"Dad phoned, saying that there was a letter for me at home. He drove down there today to pick up some things. And guess what? Edinburgh, here I come."

"You're not! You are? Edinburgh University. You've really been accepted there? I don't believe it!"

Her words were full of magic and he wanted to hug her, twirl her round, dance a jig ... but he was too sore.

Instead, he smacked the side of his head in mock disbelief and repeated, "I don't believe I'm hearing this. Not only does she follow me hundreds of miles to a remote island, but now she's following me all the way to Edinburgh. If that's not desperation, I don't know what is."

Sheleen responded with an affectionate swat on his shoulder, making him wince.

"I'll treat that remark with the contempt it deserves," she said airily, and then turned to face him. The moon had slid behind a cloud and the quiet, and the faraway light from Graham's house, merely seemed to deepen the darkness. It was difficult to read her expression.

"About -" she hesitated for a moment, " - about what we were talking about earlier ... "

"Yeah?"

"Samuel felt that I had to balance things like, well, the possibility that finding my mother, or father, may turn out to be a discovery I would be better without. On the other hand, maybe if I didn't try, then I would be sort of denying access to a part of myself."

"So, what have you decided?"

"I'm just going to pray about it. And then ... I don't know. But, if I ever meet her, it'll be to say, 'Thank you. Thank you for letting me be.' " Shivering suddenly, she zipped up her jacket. "Right, no more sentimental slush, I'm freezing. Let's run!"

"You run if you want, girl. But this guy's finished with running. Finito."

Sheleen dashed off before he could impress her with his one French word. Or was it Spanish? Smiling inside, he stooped to pick up a fallen leaf. It was curling at the edges, drying, probably beginning to turn from green to gold. Summer was over, he realised, that final summer of which it could be said, looking at the newly painted house, the mended fence, the new roof tiles, 'Graham Maclean was here and he made a difference.'

Or, that summer, it could also be said, looking at Graham Maclean, 'God came here and he made a difference.'

Also published
by
Christian Focus Publications

THE OUTSIDERS

Margaret   Smith

Stewart Steele moves to a country area from a big city
and finds that he is regarded as an outsider.

Soon he discovers that he is also an outsider from God's
kingdom.

But he is not the only one.

ISBN 1 871676 52 5

Pocket paperback   128 pages